Turning Parliament Inside Out

Turning Parliament Inside Out

PRACTICAL IDEAS FOR REFORMING CANADA'S DEMOCRACY

Edited by
Michael Chong,
Scott Simms
and Kennedy Stewart

Douglas & McIntyre

Douglas and McIntyre (2013) Ltd.
P.O. Box 219, Madeira Park, BC, V0N 2H0
www.douglas-mcintyre.com

Edited by Silas White
Cover design by Anna Comfort O'Keeffe
Text design by Mary White
Indexed by Kyla Shauer
Printed and bound in Canada
Printed on 100% recycled paper

Douglas and McIntyre (2013) Ltd. acknowledges the support of the Canada Council for the Arts, which last year invested $153 million to bring the arts to Canadians throughout the country. We also gratefully acknowledge financial support from the Government of Canada through the Canada Book Fund and from the Province of British Columbia through the BC Arts Council and the Book Publishing Tax Credit.

Cataloguing data available from Library and Archives Canada
ISBN 978-1-77162-137-3 (paper)
ISBN 978-1-77162-138-0 (ebook)

Contents

Foreword

Ed Broadbent

A s I write, virtually all of the democratic world is in a state of anxiety about the newly elected president of the United States. This anxiety is warranted because Donald Trump has shown no respect for the truth, denies the legitimacy of international law, disrespects his country's constitutional separation of powers and insults Muslims, women and those with disabilities. At the same time, however, he has promised to rectify economic injustices imposed on millions of American workers, shake up political and economic elites and disengage the country from military adventurism around the world. Trump's electoral strength was derived from a well-established Republican base but also from millions of citizens, from Appalachia to the Midwest and beyond, who had begun to feel like "strangers in their own land" (to quote the title of a recent book). His appeal to the large number of Americans thoroughly fed up with the traditional leadership of both the Republican and Democratic parties is now understood as a common-sense fact.

Equally commonplace is the view that versions of Trump's right-wing populism have been playing out for similar reasons in many European democracies. As happened in the 1930s, severe social and economic disruption is resulting in major portions of the disaffected moving not to the democratic left but to the authoritarian right. This instability, only partially related to globalization, has led to a massive rejection of traditional leaders, their parties and economic elites. Large parts of the democratic world have become concerned about the durability of their values and institutions. Once thought to be rock-solid, American, British and French democracies are now seen as more fragile. As recently as two years ago, neither their ordinary citizens nor their elites saw this coming.

It is then reasonable, not alarmist, for Canadians to consider the soundness of our democracy. It is reasonable, and indeed desirable, to look at proposed parliamentary reforms and ask, will they strengthen Parliament and add to its legitimacy as a democratic institution? Or will they hobble the effectiveness of our federal government at a time in global history when democratic leadership is especially needed?

It would be a serious mistake to see Parliament, our leaders and our political parties as the only elements affecting our economic and social well-being. But we would be equally mistaken to undervalue their importance. National political institutions and their credibility matter. The views of the leaders of Britain's largest political parties had lost the respect of major parts of the British population even before the Brexit vote. The same is true of parties and leaders in France and the US.

Americans' confidence in their congressional leaders' capacity to respond to the needs of anyone but the top 10 percent of income earners is at an all-time low. In a democracy, parliaments and their operational institutions—their leaders, MPs, parties and committees, Question Period, legislation—matter a great deal.

Is Canada's parliament responsible to its citizens, or do parties operate as leader-controlled oligarchies stifling MPs? Do women, indigenous peoples and visible minorities see themselves sufficiently in the House of Commons? Are selfies and "public engagement" being used as misleading substitutes for legislation that deals with entrenched and growing inequalities? Are the talents of individual MPs held in check or allowed to flourish during Question Period and committee work?

These questions and others are posed and answered in this book. The authors are MPs who have a deep commitment to democracy and to improving Parliament. They present a remarkable range of ideas about changes they believe will improve parliamentary democracy. I believe most of their ideas should find acceptance. And I therefore urge readers to take them seriously.

My principal point, however, is that democracy requires citizens to be actively engaged in civil society and in ongoing efforts to preserve and strengthen parliamentary institutions. Parliament's legitimacy must be earned and re-earned over time. This is especially true today, when significant inequality and instability are a growing global reality. We cannot remain complacent; reform must be ongoing. Read what these thoughtful MPs have to say. Changes to the rules and procedures of Parliament to make it more democratic for MPs are essential if Parliament and its leaders are to respond effectively to the changing needs and aspirations of ordinary Canadians. Let's get on with it.

Foreword

Preston Manning

The Parliament of Canada is the institutional embodiment and expression of the most fundamental principles of democratic governance—principles pertaining to:

1. Democratic representation: One of the basic responsibilities of elected members of Parliament is to faithfully and accurately represent the views and interests of those Canadians who elected them.
2. The rule of law: Our Constitution declares that Canada is "founded upon principles that recognize the supremacy of God and the rule of law," and one of the primary tasks of Parliament is to make statute law.
3. Fiduciary responsibility and accountability: Parliament is responsible and accountable for the collection and expenditure of public monies.

One of the purposes of embodying principles in an institution such as Parliament is to give them solidity and permanence—to ensure that those principles remain respected and practised under a variety of conditions and changing circumstances. Why then talk of "parliamentary reform," *reform* implying the need for change, changes to the institution of Parliament itself? Two reasons.

First, no institution is perfect and our Parliament is no exception. There is always room for improvement. Thus, proposals contained in this book such as those calling for modifications to Question Period, the operation of committees and the practice of petitioning should be welcomed and should receive serious consideration.

But there is a second, more fundamental reason for undertaking parliamentary reform, pointed out long ago by the great British parliamentarian Edmund Burke. An institution, Burke argued, must periodically undergo reform (he used the word *correction*) in order to conserve the very principles upon which it was founded. Why is this? It is because with the passage of time, everything above, beneath and around the institution may have changed, and it must therefore adapt to those changes or become increasingly dysfunctional and irrelevant.

At first blush, the idea of conserving the essence (the principles) of an institution by changing it may seem illogical and contradictory. But this Burkean concept was brought home to me in a very practical way by something I observed many years ago while doing community development work in northern Alberta.

Along an old back road east of Lesser Slave Lake, there once stood a huge post set in rocks with a signboard affixed to it by heavy bolts. The sign displayed one word, the name of the town of Sawridge, and an arrow pointing west. That sign did not change or move for over fifty years, no matter how hard the winds blew or how much snow fell. It always said the same thing and it always pointed in the same direction. A reliable guide to the town of Sawridge some might say.

And yet, if you followed the directions on that sign you would never get to the town of Sawridge. Why? Because although the message and the direction of that signpost never changed, everything else around it changed.

In the period following the erection of that sign, the town of Sawridge changed its name. It also changed its location, moving to higher ground after a flood in the 1930s. In addition, the roads leading to it were rerouted half a dozen times. It was the very fact that the signpost had not changed, while everything around it had, that made it an unreliable guide to anyone travelling that old road.

Thus the old signpost proclaiming the principle of democratic representation and pointing out the way to get there in 1867 may not be the most reliable guide to democratic representation in 2017. The changes in Canadian society represented by the increased diversity of our population, the demands of pluralism, advances in ways and means of ascertaining public opinion, and the advent of social media require parliamentary reforms in order to conserve Parliament's capability to provide effective democratic representation under these changed conditions.

Similarly, the old signposts defining the path to the rule of law for the nineteenth century may not be the most reliable guides to practising the rule of law in the twenty-first century. Changes in our attitudes to rights and freedoms, changes in what is required of governments in relation to the regulation of trade and commerce, changes in the nature and scope of criminal activity and policing—reform may be required to preserve Parliament's capacity to practise the rule of law under these new circumstances.

Several of the essays in this book call for reforms to alter the balance of power between the front and back benches, to break the parliamentary glass ceiling for women, and to integrate federal and provincial representation and lawmaking through an "Assembly of the Federation." All are proposals to conserve and enhance the basic principles of parliamentary democracy by making changes to help Parliament adapt to new conditions and circumstances.

Whether we ultimately agree or disagree with the proposals put forward in *Turning Parliament Inside Out*, they are all worthy of consideration, especially because they are being proposed by political practitioners rather than theorists.

I therefore wholeheartedly recommend *Turning Parliament Inside Out* to all Canadians who value the work of our Parliament.

Foreword

Bob Rae

The evidence is steadily mounting that Canadians, like virtually every public in the world, are trusting institutions less—and high on that list of skepticism is Parliament itself. Parliamentary politics have always aroused varying degrees of contempt, but things are not getting better.

There is a strong argument that any system of government has to deliver the goods. The evidence is overwhelming that over the last few decades economic growth has slowed, and its benefits have not been widely shared. No doubt this has contributed to people's scepticism about political institutions. But not all the blame can be laid at the door of the economy. Our political institutions, and how political discourse has deteriorated, have contributed to the current mood.

Voters rightly feel that there's something wrong with how our politics is working. We don't yet have the deadlock of the us, but we do have another kind of deadlock: the hard hand of too much party discipline, an inability to replace diatribe and pablum with substantive debate, and a failure to recognize that something needs to change. All players and actors in the system share equally a responsibility for what has happened. There's more than enough blame to go around.

An excessive partisanship is what Canadians see. And they don't like it. Nor are mps happy being treated like cannon fodder. Exit interviews conducted by Samara Canada serve as eloquent testimony to what retiring MPs are prepared to admit. If only they could express those thoughts more clearly while still active. Doing politics differently means changing the way Parliament works. From Question Period—where everyone is rigidly choreographed—to committees, it would be good to see change. Political discourse has increasingly become the rote repetition of the same phrases over and over again, people talking past each other, with canned answers responding to canned questions. It becomes unreal, stilted, and a substitute for thought, spontaneity and genuine debate.

Caucus discipline need not apply to every vote, and every measure before the House should not be a matter of confidence. This break-through was part of the Liberal/NDP accord signed in Ontario in 1985, but it has not been practised much since, in either minority or majority Parliaments. As I have said before, "Let the caucus be raucous." And let the House of Commons do its job in a way that respects individual members. Let committees study the subject matter of bills before they come to the House. Committees where there is real give and take, and real responsibility, will become surprisingly productive and less partisan. Members will stop screaming at each other when they realize they have something to learn from each other.

I have seen this enacted, but the examples are not legion. In the Ontario legislature, an all-party committee studied graduated licensing for young drivers and came up with a practical approach that has stood the test of time. In the House of Commons the Special Parliamentary Committee on Afghanistan broke down a lot of partisan differences, an experience deepened by a ten-day visit to Kabul, Kandahar and a number of military posts. The creation of the Parliamentary Committee on Security and Intelligence will show to what extent the executive is prepared to trust parliamentarians, and conversely to what extent parliamentarians are prepared to drop partisan combat. The next few years will reveal whether this generation of political leaders is prepared to deepen its commitment to change. For all our sakes, I hope they do.

Introduction

Michael Chong, Scott Simms
and Kennedy Stewart

Q uestion Period in the Canadian House of Commons is often described as a "bit of theatre" that gives the Canadian public a glimpse of how Ottawa works. "Don't be alarmed," reassuring reporters say. "This is not how Ottawa really works, they're just performing for the cameras." But many of us who sit in the House of Commons would argue Question Period is how Ottawa really works. For one thing, who says what, what is said, and how it is said in Question Period is completely and often ruthlessly controlled by small leadership teams dominating our political parties. For another, those asking and answering questions often do not reflect the identities or views of the wider population. Finally, the rules structuring the way we engage one another in the Chamber often negatively affect what we say. Thus, Question Period symbolizes everything rotten about Canadian politics for many members of Parliament. We also know it is only the important tip of the iceberg in terms of aspects of our political system needing change.

Written by reform-minded MPs who have put down their partisan swords long enough to each contribute a chapter on a different aspect of our work, this book explores how our national political institutions might be improved. These authors include Scott Simms and Anita Vandenbeld from the Liberal Party; Conservative MPs Michael

Chong and Michael Cooper; Niki Ashton, Nathan Cullen and Kennedy Stewart from the NDP; and Elizabeth May from the Green Party. Having sitting MPs from different parties, backgrounds and regions cooperate to produce a single book is an unusual endeavour, but one we felt to be important given the current malaise about Canadian politics. It is hoped this effort will stimulate discussion and prompt change through new government bills, opposition-day motions and private members' initiatives.

Three themes emerge from these chapters. The first theme of *party control* concerns how party leaders and their teams have come to completely dominate our political process. The second, *representation*, explores why who sits in the House of Commons and what they say are critical to the future of our country. The third theme addresses our approach to *debate* and how the way in which we speak to one another shapes the policies Ottawa produces.

Party Control

At the turn of the twentieth century, German sociologist Robert Michels spent considerable time observing the internal workings of political parties, which he wrote about in his 1911 book simply titled *Political Parties*. Michels suggests power in organizations eventually becomes concentrated in the higher echelons of their bureaucratic hierarchies, which he provocatively deems to be the "Iron Law of Oligarchy." Thus, as political parties mature, Michels suggests, party leadership teams become more stable and remote, with agenda-setting and decision-making control becoming concentrated within the leadership team.[1] While over a century has passed since Michels wrote his seminal piece, some would argue Canada's political parties have allowed themselves to succumb to Michel's "Iron Law." Whether it is the Prime Minister's Office, the office of the leader of the official Opposition, or leader's offices of smaller parties, nothing moves in Ottawa without the approval of at least one of these leadership teams—which can include the leader, whip, house leader, national caucus chair and a host of unelected officials including the chief of staff and principal secretary.

Momentarily returning to the floor of the House of Commons helps illustrate the degree to which party leadership teams control what some

---

1. Keith Dowding, ed., "Robert Michels," *Encyclopedia of Power* (London: Sage, 2011).

would claim are the most important forty-five minutes in day-to-day Canadian political life. On a typical Wednesday afternoon when the House of Commons is in session, MPs file into the Chamber, followed by the Speaker's Parade, laying of the mace, prayer and singing of "O Canada." The Speaker then says, "Let the doors be open" and members of the public and media begin to fill the gallery. Visitors first witness a few statements from members about pet causes, notable community members, high-achieving local sports clubs, or some topic that has been assigned by the leadership team. Rarely are these statements of any importance to national politics, and in the worst case, they are used to pillory opponents. Flaccid personal statements are of course preferred by party leadership teams and, as discussed later in this book, those wishing to do more with their sixty seconds are barred from doing so or punished.

The Speaker then signals it is time for "oral questions" and invites the leader of the official Opposition to kick things off. While the leader asks the prime minister a question, the PM will often look through his or her stack of carefully prepared cue cards for an answer. After the answer is announced, the Speaker names the riding of the next questioner from a list that has been provided by the party whips. For forty-five minutes questions are asked and answers are given, with applause, shouts, laughter and heckling coming from both sides. When the inquisition ends, most members file out of the House, and the Chamber returns to less entertaining regular business.

While MPs are observed by the audience up in the galleries, we also observe what is happening up there. Soon after audience members find a seat, they tend to refer to their seating charts, point out famous MPs and struggle to use their translation earpieces. Some are shushed by Commons security service. Some are told not to stand. On rare occasions, some are even ushered out after shouting at us. However, we know observing from the galleries in no way helps visitors understand what is really going on down below. The average visitor will not know MPs can only ask their 35-second question if the party leadership team has decided this particular member is the right person to put on the particular topic, or the MP is being rewarded for good behaviour, or has been given the question because someone else is being punished. They will not know that each morning MPs pitch questions to be considered, but it is the leadership team deciding which questions are asked and in what order. It is also the leadership team that almost always writes the text of the question and coaches the MP as to how it should be delivered.

Visitors soon catch on that the partisan colleagues of the member asking the question will almost always applaud no matter how the member performs and then taunt the government into providing better answers. Visitors will also see that questions are rarely directly answered and that replies are usually worded to deflect blame or insult the questioner. From above, gallery guests may also miss when very good performances prompt genuine murmurs of approval from members of other parties. When a Conservative member convincingly asks a tough question of a Liberal minister, NDP members might say to each other, "Oh, that was pretty good." On the other hand, when members flub their lines or go over the 35-second limit, they are often quietly ridiculed by their own party members. The background murmurs tell all, but you need to be on the floor to pick these up.

Directly reading scripted answers often attracts heckles from the opposition benches, not because of the answer but because of the delivery. Sometimes ministers will practise their responses to such an extent they can answer without reading their cards, which can draw whispers of approval from all sides of the House and enhance the minister's reputation for being competent. Up in the gallery, even the most senior members of the media will almost always miss the many occasions when questions or answers refer to some minor happening from a committee meeting, or something personal about an MP that prompts outrage or laughter from the entire House. It is when the whole House is yelling or guffawing that it is most clear that the Commons is not theatre put on for the audience, but rather a place where the participants can't wait to tell inside jokes.

Many argue that MPs have been reduced to this behaviour due to control by leadership teams, which extends to all aspects of parliamentary business, including who is put in charge of the most important ministries and portfolios, who sits on the frontbench, who sits on the backbench, who sits on what committee, who goes on parliamentary trips, who gives speeches in the House regarding government business, what is said in these speeches, the times and dates Parliament sits, and what resources are made available to MPs. The list goes on.

In 1924, Michels decided there was no hope for democracy and joined Benito Mussolini's National Fascist Party. While what happens in Canadian political parties is nothing close to fascism, the increasing degree of control exercised by party leadership teams is depressing for those who mistrust the concentration of power in the hands of a few. On the bright side, some scholars suggest the pull of centralization can be overcome through understanding these tendencies and cooperating to ensure power remains at least partially decentralized. One of the aims of this book is to take readers behind the emerald curtain so those interested in national politics can form a more complete picture of how party leaders dominate our work. But an equally important second objective is to suggest ways by which power can be decentralized to regular MPs and, by extension, to the general public.

Representation

A second theme of this book concerns who sits in our Parliament. Canada's House of Commons has one of the most diverse sets of elected representatives in any national legislature in the entire world, with ten indigenous members, fifteen members of South Asian descent, six MPs of Chinese ancestry, ten Muslim and six Jewish MPs, as well as six members from the LGBTQ community, eighty-eight women and ten members from the Bloc Québécois, which is dedicated to promoting Quebec sovereignty. Our parliament demonstrates just how much Canadian voters embrace supporting candidates from all backgrounds, and this diversity is something of which we should be very proud.

However, a closer look reveals Parliament still does not mirror Canadian society. For example, women hold just 26 percent of the seats in the House of Commons while making up half of the overall population. So even though the House of Commons is diverse, this broader array of MPs is a fairly recent phenomenon and many groups are still underrepresented.

The first words uttered by a woman in the House of Commons were spoken by Grey Southeast MP Agnes Macphail, who began her March 29, 1922, maiden speech with "Mr. Speaker, I think what women really want today is perfect equality with men."[2] Before 1921, the male-only House of Commons would speak *about* women and even *for* women, but they could not speak *as* women because women were banned

---

2. Canada, *House of Commons Debates* (29 March 1922), 14th Parliament, 1st session, 1:479, http://parl.canadiana.ca/view/oop. debates_HOC1401_01/493?r=0&s=4.

from standing as candidates. Moving forward to 1957, Prime Minister John Diefenbaker appointed Ellen Fairclough as Canada's first female cabinet minister. Also in 1957, Progressive Conservative MP Douglas Jung became the first person of Chinese heritage to sit in the House of Commons. Despite significant contributions to Canada including military service, Chinese Canadians were not enfranchised until 1947.

Another Canadian first occurred on September 13, 1968. No indigenous person had spoken in the House of Commons until MP Len Marchand spoke these words in his reply to the speech from the throne:

> I am the first Indian to sit as a member of this house and I am conscious of my responsibilities...I have an obligation which I could not escape if I wished to, and that is my obligation to my fellow Indians...Hon. members know that the situation of many Indian families is deplorable. We all know that in respect of income, standards of health and living conditions many Indians are living below that standard of respectability in this country. They are isolated from their fellow Canadians and shut off from many aspects of Canadian life...The efforts to bring them into the world of today and hold their rightful place in Canada must continue.[3]

The politics of presence matters not just for what is said, but for the added power that comes when words come from the lips of those who have been affected or will be affected by government policies. Only four Métis people, including Louis Riel, had been elected as members of Parliament prior to 1968. And it was not until 1979 that Peter Ittinuar would speak as the first Inuk MP. Those attending the 41st Parliament would likely have been struck by the number of young people asking and answering questions during Question Period, including the youngest man and woman ever elected to the House. In his first parliamentary question, asked on June 7, 2011, nineteen-year-old Pierre-Luc Dusseault asked what the Conservative government intended to do to help students living below the poverty line. Two days later, twenty-year-old

---

3. Canada, *House of Commons Debates* (13 September 1968), 28th Parliament, 1st session, 1:33, http://parl.canadiana.ca/view/oop. debates_HOC2801_01/35?r=0&s=1.

Laurin Liu from Rivière-des-Mille-Îles asked how the government was going to address climate change.

Who sits in the House of Commons is important not only for symbolic reasons, but also to ensure all Canadians can fairly contribute to our policy-making process. Where outright bans of people with particular ancestries, beliefs or practices are no longer the norm, that the composition of Canada's parliament still does not reflect our population raises important questions about why this might be the case and what can be done to address this imbalance. Here again it is worth looking at the role political parties play in determining who participates in formal national politics. Leadership team control extends from who is allowed to stand for candidacy during elections to elected life, when MPs are expected to continue pleasing their party leadership teams.

Leadership team control is supported by legislation such as the *Canada Elections Act*, which requires candidates to be endorsed by the party leader before they can run for that party during an election. Likewise, the *Parliament of Canada Act* further entrenches leadership control by empowering leadership teams to kick sitting MPs out of their parties at their discretion. One of the most important recent debates about party control played out in the 41st Parliament when in December 2013, Conservative MP Michael Chong introduced Bill C-559: *An Act to Amend the Canada Elections Act and the Parliament of Canada Act*, more commonly known as the *Reform Act*. Chong introduced the *Reform Act* in an effort to reduce the power of party leadership teams using two main measures: first, prospective candidates would only be required to receive the approval of constituency-level party officials and not the party leader to stand in an election; second, decision-making control of issues such as determining when MPs are kicked out of the party, electing national caucus chairs, and reviewing/removing the party leader would be shifted from the party leadership team to a vote of the full caucus of MPs.

The bill generated significant support within and outside Parliament but appeared to be doomed due to opposition from Prime Minister Stephen Harper as well as some frontbench MPs from other parties. After wide consultation, Chong revised the bill so it no longer mandated these changes upon adoption but rather upon approval by each party caucus. The revised bill, now numbered C-586, passed through the House of Commons and Senate, receiving royal assent on June 23, 2015.

The changes brought in by the *Reform Act* meant all recognized parties were required to vote on the provisions within C-586 at the first official caucus meeting after the October 19, 2015, general election. To the disappointment of many, the Conservative Party adopted only a few of the measures contained in the act, and the Liberal and NDP caucuses adopted none (although the Liberals and the NDP already empower MPs to elect their caucus chair). The *Reform Act* saga highlights the power that party leadership teams have over regular MPs. It also shows just how hard it is for MPs to change our governing institutions—especially if they're for backbenchers. The most optimistic view is that the process by which the bill was passed demonstrates that cooperation and compromise are possible among reformers. Those who want change can take lessons from C-586 and keep trying.

Debate

Anyone viewing Question Period or other debates in the House may be excused for being bored. Many discussions are so tightly scripted by leadership teams that little of interest is ever uttered. The ad nauseam repetition of three or four talking points on why a bill is good or bad for a few hours would drive anyone to seek refuge from the tedium. This is a shame because the diversity of views and backgrounds represented by the 338 Canadians elected to speak on the floor of the House of Commons could make for a much more enlightening discussion. Every once in a while a ray of light shines through the clouds of backroom-scripted speeches to illuminate matters of great importance to Canadians: words about who we are and what we perhaps could be.

Observers who stuck around for a few minutes after Question Period on May 22, 1990, witnessed a speech about one of the most important issues in Canadian politics. On this date, Conservative MP Lucien Bouchard rose on a point of privilege to explain why he was quitting the Conservative caucus after a report was released outlining concessions Prime Minister Brian Mulroney was prepared to make to pass the faltering Meech Lake Accord:

> I do not doubt Mr. Mulroney's intentions but by conferring this status on the report, the government is in fact forming an alliance with the very parties that would impose humiliating terms on Quebec...I disapprove of it utterly, and I see

no alternative but to leave this government—be it with feelings of pain and anguish—as well as the Conservative caucus,
to sit as an independent member.[4]

Bouchard's speech led to the creation of a party dedicated to fundamentally changing Canada as we know it, the Bloc Québécois. It also
illustrates how the House of Commons can create space for all viewpoints to be publicly aired and for ideas to take shape as to what Canada
is and what it means to be Canadian. Unlike other countries, where such
a declaration could lead to conflict or even civil war, our parliament has
the capacity to accommodate these tough discussions.

On December 12, 1995, Bloc MP Maurice Dumas faced the Speaker
and stated, "Quebecers always felt that Confederation was a pact
between the four original provinces and basically an agreement between
the two founding nations. Thus, any constitutional amendment requires
Quebec's approval, as one of the two founding nations." And on May 16,
1996, Liberal MP Jack Iyerak Anawak from Nunatsiaq contributed a new
twist: "Mr. Speaker, whenever I hear about the two founding nations I
think of Christopher Columbus stumbling on to America by mistake
thinking he was somewhere else and finding out there were already
people here in 1492. Therefore when I hear about the two founding
nations I think of the Inuit and the Indian people of North America."

On November 25, 1997, however, Reform Party MP Cliff Breitkreuz
from Yellowhead, Alberta, rose to express his view of Canada as a single
nation: "There is no constitutional basis or constitutional history to
give support and credibility to the concepts of two founding nations
and distinct society. No Fathers of Confederation, not even the French-
speaking Fathers of Confederation, said anything of two nations and
distinct society." A fourth idea of Canada was heard on the morning of
June 4, 2010, when Conservative MP Colin Mayes from British Columbia
expressed the idea of Canada being founded by three nations: "The three
founding nations of Canada—the aboriginals, the francophones and the
anglophones—should be recognized as the nations that have placed the
foundation stones for our freedoms and rights."

---

4. Canada, *House of Commons Debates* (22 May 1990), 34th
Parliament, 2nd session, 9:11663, http://parl.canadiana.ca/view/oop.
debates_HOC3402_09/245?r=0&s=1.

These snippets provide a glimpse of what the House of Commons could look like under different circumstances, where "talking at" progressed to "talking to" other MPs. By speaking their minds, MPs could contribute their expertise and might better reflect the will of their constituents. They would undoubtedly generate more controversy and interest through the media and social media, but would also present a more engaging approach to the public. Governments wouldn't always win debates, nor would the opposition. Legislation might have to be altered after hearing the spectrum of options from those with different views. After all, democracy is—and should be—messy. At the very least, our neat and tidy House of Commons could use fewer scripted speeches and a bit more character.

Chapter Overview

The themes outlined in this introduction—party control, representation and debate—run through the chapters that follow. Readers will notice some overlap, discontinuity and variation in the degree to which reform is required and which reforms might work best. Far from being problematic, this messiness matches our hope for the book to reflect how things work in Ottawa. The final chapter attempts to tie this all together and suggests how such reforms might be best realized.

Elizabeth May kicks us off with a trip through time. She illustrates how the role of ordinary MPs and minor parties has been greatly reduced, providing examples from her time as a parliamentarian and senior staffer in the Progressive Conservative Mulroney government. May suggests a better balance can be struck by requiring votes on important procedural issues to come out of the backrooms and onto the floor of the House.

Conservative MP Michael Cooper presents his case for reforming Question Period. Arguing that it needs tweaking rather than a complete overhaul, Cooper suggests a certain amount of banter and heckling benefits parliamentary debate. He goes on to outline how decorum might be improved, including by having the Speaker more frequently reprimand bad behaviour, changing the length and nature of how questions are asked and answered, banning clapping, reducing the use of party-sanctioned speaking lists and exploring the use of special Question Periods.

New Democratic Party MP Kennedy Stewart shares experience gained from shepherding a private member's motion through the House of Commons to explore the benefits of returning power to the backbench. He outlines how private members' business once dominated the parliamentary agenda, but now party leadership teams control all but a very small portion of what occurs in the House. Stewart shows how bringing electronic petitions to Canada's parliament exposed the crushing power of leadership teams as well as what cross-partisan cooperation can achieve.

Reform Act author Michael Chong looks at how to rebalance power between party leaders and elected MPs through restructuring parliamentary committees. After arguing the primary role of committees is to hold the government to account, Chong compares the current Canadian committee system to the British system. He concludes that Canadians would be better served if there were fewer committees and if the power to appoint committee members and chairs was removed from party leaders and given to ordinary MPs.

NDP MP Nathan Cullen provides a rollicking account of his first parliamentary speech. His story highlights the importance of striking the right balance between doing what the party tells you to do and being true to yourself. Sharing lessons he has learned from First Nations leaders, Cullen argues MPs should agree to bring in reforms to make the House of Commons a place of dialogue and that if we don't, we may be forced to do so by frustrated citizens.

Liberal MP Anita Vandenbeld throws a stone at the parliamentary glass ceiling. She argues that while there is real cause to celebrate Prime Minister Justin Trudeau's decision to appoint a gender-balanced cabinet, Canada still lags far behind other countries internationally when it comes to women's legislative representation, and that women face different challenges than men do after being elected to office. Vandenbeld's suggestions range from incentivizing parties to select more women candidates, empowering Elections Canada to become more involved in the nomination process and implementing measures to increase inter-party cooperation among women MPs.

NDP MP Niki Ashton takes on the issue of youth apathy, arguing that the downward trend of young people participating in electoral politics may have been changed forever by the 2015 election. Drawing on examples from her riding, which contains many rural and remote communities, Ashton explores the power of social media and political action taken by youth outside the voting booth. She calls on parties to do more to build on what she sees as an emerging opportunity to make politics more relevant for all Canadians.

Veteran Liberal MP Scott Simms looks at how we might use parliamentary institutions to better utilize talent on provincial backbenches through a new institution he calls the "Assembly of the Federation." Building on the current "Council of the Federation," where provincial first ministers meet to discuss shared interests, and his firsthand observations of the Council of Europe, Simms proposes that provincial backbenchers would come to Ottawa to produce motions that would then go to the House of Commons for debate. This new "house of sober first thought" could go a long way to increasing decentralization and grassroots input into national policy—and by extension, allow provincial backbenchers a route to empowerment beyond what provincial leaders provide.

The Story of the Book

It is perhaps worth explaining how this collection of essays came about—after all, it is not every day that a gaggle of politicians of different stripes comes together to produce a book. The soil was tilled in 2011 when the lottery to decide the order of precedence for private members' business placed Kennedy Stewart in the 90th and Michael Chong in the 123rd positions—thus arranging simultaneous discussions of Stewart's electronic petitions private member's motion and Chong's *Reform Act*. Eventually, these debates led reform-minded MPs of all parties to engage in a wider discussion about how things could be changed in order to counter the crushing force of partisanship and pass both measures through the House of Commons.

Discussions of reform continued to percolate throughout the 41st Parliament. Just prior to the House rising for a final time in 2015, Stewart approached Chong about doing a book together if re-elected. After both survived the gruelling seventy-eight-day campaign and were sworn into the 42nd Parliament, Chong suggested Liberal veteran MP Scott Simms, who was keen to join, as a third member to round out the editorial team. The three of us decided the book should only include sitting MPs and would generally avoid discussing electoral reform, as that topic was being fully covered by a special committee. In addition, we agreed that any proceeds would be donated to Samara Canada, a non-partisan charity dedicated to increasing civic engagement in Canada. Needing to secure a publisher, Stewart suggested Douglas & McIntyre due to its reputation for publishing political books such as Brad Lavigne's *Building the Orange Wave* and Susan Delacourt's *Shopping for Votes*. Stewart called D&M's general number and to his surprise, company president Howard White picked up the phone after three rings. Within about fifteen minutes, Stewart and White agreed to move forward with the book.

We began to recruit other authors. Our original idea was to have two Conservatives, two Liberals, two NDPers, one member of the Bloc, and Elizabeth May representing the Green Party. We agreed the book should be as regionally and gender balanced as possible, and that one chapter should be written by an indigenous MP. Recruitment did not prove easy. A number of MPs did not reply to our invitation, others agreed immediately but dropped out and others started but never finished chapters. This is all understandable given the pressures of the job. We are grateful to all who considered contributing and very grateful to those who stuck it out.

The final stage in the process was to secure a cross-partisan set of preface authors who would add gravitas to the book. Despite their hectic schedules, Ed Broadbent, Preston Manning and Bob Rae enthusiastically agreed to provide prefaces. The D&M team, including Peter Robson, Silas White, Amanda Growe, Mary White, Kathy Vanderlinden, Patricia Wolfe, Brianna Cerkiewicz and Kyla Shauer, helped to mould all the contributions into enjoyable and provocative pieces. Coordinating editor Jeanette Ashe helped immeasurably. Overall, we hope this book not only provides food for thought, but also shows it is possible for politicians of different stripes to come together and have a positive impact on Canadian politics. We also hope that it will lead to parliamentary reform as well as similar projects in the future. We only have one national parliament, so it is up to us all to make it work better for Canadians.

On February 1, just as this book was about to go to press, Prime Minister Trudeau declared that despite his election promise to make the 2015 election "the last federal election using first-past-the-post," months of work by a special House of Commons committee, two separate public engagement and consultation exercises, numerous MP town hall meetings and one cross-country ministerial tour, electoral reform was no longer on the table because "there is no consensus among Canadians on how, or even whether, to reform our electoral system." Where authors included in this text will have different views about this decision by the prime minister, the fact that the next election will be conducted using single member plurality rules puts additional pressure on MPs to work together to reform other aspects of our parliamentary system. Where we would all agree the electoral formula is a very important component of our national democracy, there are other parts that can and should be reformed before the next election.

Westminster Parliamentary Democracy: Where Some MPs Are More Equal Than Others

Elizabeth May

The roots of Canada's parliament can be traced back hundreds if not thousands of years. As we all learn in school, the cradle of democracy was ancient Greece. The idea was new: a shared participation in the life of a city was expected. Pericles made this clear in existential terms: "A man who does not participate in the life of the city we do not think really lives at all." Of course, that Athenian democracy would not be recognized as democratic in the twenty-first century. Slavery was legal, women were chattel and minority rights had no protections. Nevertheless, the fundamentals of political philosophy, of the ethics of living together in a society, were established by great philosophers like Pericles, Socrates and Plato. The very idea that a society could be governed not by a king but by its citizens owes its origins to ancient Greece.

Canada's parliament owes its more specific configurations to the Westminster parliamentary system as it evolved in England. The first humbling of a king before his subjects was on the fields of Runnymede in 1215. King John had angered the lords of his court by passing laws that affected their property without consulting them. When he signed the Magna Carta, it was an extraordinary realignment of the rights, responsibilities and powers of a monarch. For the first time, the king was forced to admit that he was not above the law, but had an obligation to consult with a council of lords and peers.

This obligation to consult evolved over time into the Westminster parliamentary model now found in Commonwealth countries around the world. The chamber of lords became the House of Lords in the UK and the Senate in Canada. In the fourteenth century, the king asked the commoners to elect a speaker from among themselves so their concerns could be voiced directly to the king. The lower house of commoners eventually became the House of Commons. Those closest to the king, those privy to his secrets, laid the basis for what evolved into a Privy Council—or cabinet. It is this connection to the monarch that continues with the swearing-in of cabinet members at Rideau Hall. The "PC" designation after the names of current and past Privy Councillors denotes that they are to be trusted with the secrets of the nation.

It was not until the Industrial Revolution that the role of the monarch became entirely ceremonial. As Canada was establishing what we thought were the first democratic institutions in North America, with the first democratically elected legislature convening in Halifax in 1758, we were naturally modelling our governance on England's. We missed that there were already systems of democratic governance in North America. For over nine hundred years, the Haudenosaunee Confederacy had operated under the Great Law of Peace. As John Ralston Saul explains in *A Fair Country*, Canada could have looked to this extraordinary model, which balanced male rule with the matriarchs of the society.[5] One can even make the case, as Saul does, that the words of the British North America Act, which created an independent Canada in 1867, owe much to the sensibilities of the Great Law of Peace.

Since 1867, our democracy has evolved in many ways. It would be easy to assume that this evolution has favoured increasing the level of accountability, democratic legitimacy and respect for all people. Women got the vote. Japanese Canadians got the vote. Indigenous Canadians finally got the right to vote. In 1982, under then–prime minister Pierre Trudeau, Canadians finally received constitutionally protected rights in a repatriated Canadian Constitution. The Canadian Charter of Rights and Freedoms (part of the Constitution) has advanced the rights of

---

5. John Ralston Saul, *A Fair Country: Telling Truths About Canada* (Toronto: Viking Canada, 2008).

marginalized groups within Canada, including First Nations, LGBTQ people, people with disabilities, women and refugees.

It is true that in 2016 Canada is much more a recognized functional democracy than we were in 1867. But there is one aspect of our evolution that runs counter to enhanced democracy. In one area, the role of members of Parliament has been made increasingly unaccountable. Whereas in our initial parliamentary gatherings, MPs were seen as equal—with the prime minister "first among equals"—the growth in the power of political parties has steadily reduced the scope of action of individual members of Parliament. Some of this has been incremental and accomplished through unwritten rules. Some has been the result of highly specific changes in standing orders and legislation. The general drift has been toward centralizing the powers of the executive (prime minister and Privy Council) at the expense of the legislative.

Political Parties: Origins, Legitimacy and Power
Political parties are not mentioned in the Canadian Constitution, neither in the 1867 version of the British North America Act, nor our 1982 Constitution Act. In 1861, John Stuart Mill published *Considerations on Representative Government*. He described the essence of our system. We hold to a system of responsible government, meaning not that the government behaves responsibly in some normative sense, but rather that individual MPs are elected to be responsible to their constituents. MPs are to work for their constituents by holding government to account. In Mill's *Considerations on Representative Government*, political parties are not even mentioned.

In Westminster parliamentary democracy, political parties are not an essential ingredient. I have often said that if I were to invent democracy from scratch, I would not have invented political parties. Their existence is not a necessary, or even desirable, part of responsible government.

Initially, political parties in the British parliament were loose factions. In the seventeenth century, the derogatory terms *Whig* and *Tory* emerged to characterize the general philosophy of those who tended toward more liberal or conservative ideals. They tended to form around a particularly strong leader. Running for Parliament, out on the hustings, a candidate could make his (no "her" in those days) political philosophy clear by declaring an allegiance with Gladstone over Disraeli.

Canada's first prime minister, Sir John A. Macdonald, ran under the Conservative Party banner, but he exerted almost no control over members of Parliament within his own caucus. Macdonald referred to them as "loose fish." Candidates for office, running for seats in our House of Commons, were on the ballot listed solely by their name. Political party affiliations were not included on the ballots from 1867 until 1974. We are so accustomed in Canada to the dominance of political labels or "brands," and to the characteristics of local candidates being a minor element in the gladiatorial contest between national parties and their leaders, that it is something of a surprise to realize how recently political parties became dominant.

The key change was made in legislation in 1970, but the ballots did not change until the general election of 1974. For the first time, political parties had to register with Elections Canada, field at least fifty candidates across the country and have the leader of the party authorize each candidate's nomination papers in order to be listed on the ballot under that party's banner. This new system also imposed financial reporting requirements on political parties and many other positive steps toward accountability. It also had the unintended consequence of increasing the ability of the party's leader to hold power, and the impact of threats and retribution should a candidate or sitting MP earn the leader's ire. Without the leader's signature on the nomination papers, a candidate would be disqualified from running. This was the case even if that candidate was duly nominated through an open and fair nomination race at the local level. In this way, top-down control by the party leader over nominations was introduced.

I have heard several explanations for the addition of the political party name on the ballot. It has been suggested that in some contests, candidates had identical names. Listing the name of their party affiliation prevented confusion. Another is that as individual electoral districts grew in population, the ability to have a personal sense of the candidate was reduced. Identification with a national platform was part of voter information intended to remedy the growing distance between personal knowledge of the candidate and the ballot.

Whatever the rationale, the effect was to significantly increase the power of a party leader over his or her caucus. No more "loose fish"! Any sign of veering from the party line could be met with swift and effective retribution. Another change that occurred through the latter half of the twentieth century was a greater structure of the internal party process. Whereas in the past, party leaders had been chosen from within their own parliamentary caucus, as is the case in most Commonwealth countries, in Canada our party culture began to follow that of the United States.

Having removed themselves from the dictates of a monarch, the American founders put limitations on the power of those they would elect. The US Constitution separates the powers of the executive and legislative branches to create checks and balances. Within the Canadian system, a prime minister whose party has a majority of the seats in the House controls both the executive (prime minister and cabinet) and legislative (the majority of MPs in the House) branches.

This is also true for the Westminster system in other Commonwealth nations, but due to the Canadian party system a prime minister in Canada has more power than a UK or Australian or New Zealand PM while also having more power than a US president. Political scientist Donald Savoie identified this in his study on centralization of executive powers.[6] By electing a party leader through internal party rules, a non-parliamentary process at national conventions, the Canadian political culture makes it much harder for a party leader to be replaced than in other Westminster systems. Recall that Margaret Thatcher was replaced by her caucus. More recently, Australia's Labour party dumped a leader who was prime minister at the time, Kevin Rudd, for Julia Gillard. Before the next election Rudd returned the favour, replacing her.

It makes more sense that in a governmental system where the prime minister is "first among equals," the selection of that leader takes place within the parliamentary caucus of his or her equals. We have mixed up our systems. The US, with its separation of powers, has a direct election for president. Every voting American receives a ballot with the names of all contenders for the presidency, whereas in Canada only the local constituents of party leaders will ever have a chance to directly vote for one of them (to be an MP, not prime minister/leader).

Ironically, what appears more democratic—a public convention with delegates from across the country waving placards and cheering for their favourite—creates a more imperial leadership model than a behind-closed-doors gathering of elected MPs choosing to oust their leader. A parliamentary caucus in Canada cannot replace its leader.

---

6. Donald Savoie, *Governing from the Centre: The Concentration of Power in Canadian Politics* (Toronto: University of Toronto Press, 1999), 107–8.

Only the membership through a confidence vote and a convention can do that. In the process, the power of the individual MP is further eroded in relation to the power of the political party, and the particular power of that party leader. The harder it is to remove party leaders, the greater the scope for their abuse of power.

Political scientist Hugo Cyr has proposed that following an election, the House of Commons should vote to elect a prime minister. This could take place between the election of the Speaker and the speech from the throne. This is neither radical nor undemocratic. We have a system of government in which the election of members of Parliament determines which party will form government. The party that forms government has already chosen its leader under its internal constitution, through a big US-style convention. Cyr believes it is important to have such a vote even if it is only symbolic—to confirm a party leader as prime minister—in order to underscore our system of government. He cites the fact that in a recent poll, over half of Canadians mistakenly thought we directly elect a prime minister.[7]

As the role of political parties became more pronounced in Parliament, another trend emerged: bigger parties took steps to expand their clout, restricting the role of smaller parties. Since 1921, Canada has been a multi-party democracy. Some of those parties have been relegated to history. The year 1921 saw the rise of the Progressive Party and United Farmers. The Co-operative Commonwealth Federation, or CCF, founded in 1932, went on to become a permanent part of the political landscape as the New Democratic Party. Reform rose up and challenged the Progressive Conservative Party, only to morph into the Alliance party and successfully slay the older conservative party through a forced amalgamation. With more political parties and more diversity in the House, the old-line liberal and conservative parties felt the competition.

In 1963, Parliament passed a new rule that gave parties with more than twelve sitting MPs additional financial resources. The bigger parties argued that it was appropriate to allocate public funds to top up the salaries of their leaders, including whips, critics and committee chairs, as well as to staff a party research bureau. Had I been in Parliament at the time, I would have pointed out that none of this is a legitimate

---

7. ERRE-11 (27 July 2016) at 14:25 (Hugo Cyr's testimony).

use of public funds. The Library of Parliament researches questions for any and every MP. If the work is not being prepared fast enough, then increase the budget for the library. The change went through with barely a murmur. In the process, a new concept was invented: the "recognized party." Only recognized parties were entitled to additional financial resources. In all other respects, members of smaller parties and independents had the same rights as MPs in larger parties.

Over time, with no further changes of the rules, it became practice to exclude MPs from parties with fewer than twelve seats from parliamentary standing committees, time in Question Period and use of various parliamentary procedures, such as supply day motions. Exceptions were made. Shortly after the new rules came in, when the Ralliement Créditiste split off from the Social Credit Party, the Social Credit Party dropped to eleven sitting members. Still, it was allowed to be seated as a recognized party and had access to the procedures—if not the money—it had once had. But the larger parties continued to undercut smaller parties.

In 1990, the Bloc Québécois took a run at the argument. The Bloc went up against the actual rule that parties with fewer than twelve seats should not have access to additional funds. The Bloc asked the Speaker directly to rule that it had a right to additional monies. The Speaker at the time, John Fraser, denied the request but did not suggest small parties had no rights:

> It is important to note that the decision does not mean that the members in this group are impeded from full participation in the work of the House or that they are being deprived of support necessary to represent their constituents adequately...To date these efforts [to get research funds from the Board of Internal Economy] have proven unsuccessful, but it is a long and dangerous leap to conclude from there that the basic rights and privileges of those Members are somehow being abrogated. A search of the Debates will show, on the contrary, that the honourable Member for Shefford and his colleagues have been extended every courtesy by this House and that the Chair has safeguarded their

participation in ways that are fully in keeping with our procedure and practices.[8]

Despite Speaker Fraser's defence of "basic rights and privileges" for MPs
in smaller parties, by 1994 the presumption that MPs in parties with
fewer than twelve members were to be relegated to rear corners in the
back of the House and be denied daily time in Question Period had
become solidified. In the 1993 election, the NDP fell below twelve seats.
On June 1, 1994, Manitoba NDP MP Bill Blaikie, a skilled and passionate
orator, made a detailed and well-researched plea to the Speaker. Blaikie
argued that the 1963 finance rules should not be used to keep the nine
NDP MPs from being able to fully participate in the life of the House.

> The real conventions of this place and the conventional
> wisdom are not always the same. The recent conventional
> wisdom has been that the twelve-member threshold for
> party status is a hard and fast rule understood in an unam-
> biguous way by all concerned. My point today is that the
> question of party status has in fact been governed by
> unwritten convention and practice and that the only thing
> that is hard and fast is the question of which parties qualify
> for certain moneys...
>
> John C. Courtney, a political scientist who published a
> paper on party recognition in March 1978 in a volume of the
> *Canadian Journal of Political Science*, explained the devel-
> opment of the misreading of the twelve-member threshold
> very effectively: "Technically the twelve-member threshold
> in the 1963 act and parliamentary procedure had nothing to
> do with one another, yet the timing of the events was virtu-
> ally certain to produce a combination that would lead to the
> injection of the phrase 'recognized membership of twelve or
> more persons in the House of Commons' into future debates
> over regulations and statutes dealing with political parties.
> The term, indeed more specifically the number, would gradu-
> ally assume an authenticity of its own."

---

8. Canada, *House of Commons Debates* (13 December 1990), 34th
Parliament, 2nd session, 12:16703-4, http://parl.canadiana.ca/view/oop.
debates_HOC3402_12/1?r=0&s=1

The view that the twelve-member threshold constitutes a hard and fast rule in law about party status in this House is in fact an illusion. However, in an illustration of the old maximum [*sic*] that hard cases make bad law, misapplications designed to deal with divided and/or new parties are now sideswiping the NDP in the absence of an appropriate will to discern the difference between some previous situations and the situation we find ourselves in at the moment.[9]

Speaker Gilbert Parent essentially sidestepped making a ruling on the merit of Blaikie's point of order. He ruled that it was up to the House itself to decide if the nine NDP MPs could have any special status, be allowed to be seated together, or recognized as a party for Question Period:

A situation such as that now facing the House must be resolved by the House itself. It is not one where the Speaker ought by himself to take a position where any group of members might feel that their interests as a group or a party have been prejudiced. Nor should the Speaker be put in the position where he must decide, to the advantage or to the disadvantage of any group or party, matters affecting the character of existences of a party, for this surely would signify that the Speaker has taken what is almost a political decision, a decision where the question involves the rights and privileges of the House itself.[10]

Over time, with no vote or debate, by accretion the rights of MPs in smaller parties had been reduced. These "rules" had become accepted as convention. No one disputes the right of MPs from parties duly registered as national parties by Elections Canada, but with fewer than twelve elected members, to sit as members under their party identification.

---

9. Canada, *House of Commons Debates*. 35th Parliament, 1st session, Hansard 076, June 1, 1994, http://www.parl.gc.ca/HousePublications/Publication.aspx?Language=E&Mode=1&Parl=35&Ses=1&DocId=2332331

10. *Canada, House of Commons Debates*. 35th Parliament, 1st session, Hansard 087, June 16, 1994, http://www.parl.gc.ca/HousePublications/Publication.aspx?Language=E&Mode=1&Parl=35&Ses=1&DocId=2332341

Yet, even that is occasionally assailed, as members of smaller parties are sloppily referred to as "independents."

Given Speaker Parent's 1994 ruling, the only way for smaller parties to get equal treatment is if the bigger parties cede that to them. So the NDP, having begged for fair treatment when it was down to nine seats, was rebuffed by the larger Bloc Québécois. No surprise that when the Bloc dropped below twelve seats the now-larger NDP was unsympathetic.

Running directly against the principle that all MPs are equal, suddenly MPs from bigger parties were a whole lot more equal than others. Some might argue that there is no offence in this. As the role of parties becomes more prominent, what right do smaller parties—such as the Green Party, for which I am the sole MP—have to take up space in Parliament?

Here is where we need to return to fundamentals. No one would find objectionable the assertion that every Canadian is equal to every other Canadian. So too is every electoral district equal to every other electoral district. The job description for MPs is found in only one place—the Constitution of Canada. As an important law for a representative democracy, the Constitution has little to say about the role of an MP. It says only that MPs are elected to represent constituents. As the Constitution says nothing about political parties, it is a distortion of Westminster parliamentary democracy to have two tiers of MPs other than those in the executive (cabinet).

The job of an MP is to hold government (the executive) to account. For most of our history, this was understood. In the past, even those MPs who were elected as part of the party that formed government were still expected to ask tough questions and hold government to account. These principles, now long forgotten, were so robust that if a backbench member of a governing party was elevated to the Privy Council to become part of the cabinet, there was an expectation that he would step down to run in a by-election. The electorate was entitled to decide if it wanted an MP whose primary task was to work for constituents and hold government to account or to be part of government. The role of part of the legislature of holding the executive to account was more significant than party affiliation. Crossing the floor to change parties was not seen as a reason for holding a by-election, though joining cabinet was.[11]

The next big shift in parliamentary rules to further squash parties in opposition came as a result of an Alliance party effort at procedural monkey business in the late 1990s. Up until the year 2002, members of Parliament of all parties had the right to put forward amendments at "report stage." The trouble started in 1999. The issue at hand was the Nisga'a Treaty. Indian and Northern Affairs minister Robert Nault took the long and complicated treaty through the legislative process. Once through first and second Reading, having completed its review in committee, it came to the House for report stage.

It was at report stage that the Alliance party used its rights to put forward amendments in an attempt to derail the treaty. It moved over seven hundred amendments. They were described as "substantive amendments" in contrast to deletions, but the proposals were far from any layperson's understanding of "substantive." Removal of semicolons, small wording changes—any and all allowable mischief to delay and protest the long-awaited treaty.

The Liberal government of Jean Chrétien, over a period of years, later changed the parliamentary rules to prevent such an abuse of report-stage amending rights. The solution was to change the standing orders such that members of Parliament who had an opportunity through their party to put forward amendments in committee had no such right to put forward further substantive amendments at report stage. That created the unintended reality that the only members of Parliament with an opportunity to put forward substantive amendments at report stage were those who were in parties smaller than twelve or were sitting as independents, because we had no representation on committees. MPs in smaller parties were therefore the only ones with the right to put forward amendments other than deletions at report stage.

I think I was the first MP to notice this. I used it effectively on bill after bill put forward by Stephen Harper's Conservative majority, most notably in fighting omnibus budget bill C-38 in spring 2012. To confront the destruction of Canadian environmental laws, I moved over four hundred amendments at report stage, and with full support from the Liberal, NDP and Bloc members, I fought the bill with twenty-four

11. Brent Rathgeber, *Irresponsible Government: The Decline of Parliamentary Democracy in Canada* (Toronto: Dundurn, 2014), 94–96.

straight hours of voting. My goal was not mere delay. I hoped that by creating leverage, I could get the Conservative government to agree to one or two amendments and thus lessen the damage of Bill C-38. In the end, C-38 went from first reading to royal assent without a single amendment. Even drafting errors were left.

In the fall session of 2012, then–government House leader Peter Van Loan raised a point of order with the Speaker. In what was a historical "first," a political party with a majority of seats in the House sought to reduce the rights and privileges of a single MP from a party with fewer than twelve seats. Van Loan proposed that my amendments not be allowed to proceed at report stage in the future. His innovative notion was that one amendment should be put to a test vote and if it failed, the rest of my proposed amendments should be deemed to have failed, too. Van Loan complained to the Speaker that one MP should not have the ability to "hold the House hostage."

But Speaker Andrew Scheer refused to disallow my rights. He ruled that it is the role of MPs to participate in the deliberative process of passing legislation. He quoted former speaker Fraser in promoting a "parliamentary democracy, not a so-called executive democracy, nor a so-called administrative democracy." Speaker Scheer ruled that as long as I had had no chance to present amendments in committee, I could not be denied the right to present amendments at report stage.[12]

This hint at a loophole was seized upon by the Conservatives. Rather than go through the long process of actually changing the rules of the House, as the Chrétien Liberals had done, they found a shortcut. They drafted a motion for every committee to offer smaller-party and independent MPs the "opportunity" to present amendments during clause-by-clause consideration of every bill. With strict timelines to give these MPs forty-eight hours' notice of upcoming clauses, a requirement to submit amendments in the same window, and permission to speak briefly to each amendment (most committee chairs decided one minute was sufficient) but not to move them or vote on them, it was hardly an equal opportunity. Nor was it one I wanted. Report stage can only occur one bill at a time, since it takes place in the House itself, whereas clause-by-clause review of bills can and does happen simultaneously in committee rooms in various buildings in the parliamentary precinct.

12. Canada, *House of Commons Debates*, 41st Parliament, 1st session, vol. 146, No. 197 (12 December 2012), 15:50–15:55.

The sleight of hand used to change the process by which bills move through the House without actually amending the standing rules relied on the misuse of a key principle: that committees are the masters of their own proceedings. Therefore, simultaneous and identical motions would suddenly emerge from each committee—of course imposed by the Prime Minister's Office with instructions that they be adopted. Once the identical motion had been passed in every standing committee, I was summoned with the "invitation."

When committees happened to be holding clause-by-clause examination of different bills at the same time, I literally ran from one committee to another to try to speak to my amendments before they would go down to ritual and routine defeat. I raced to the Environment Committee to try to defend my amendment to disallow oil and gas activity inside Sable Island National Park, only to arrive after the committee had defeated it. On one bill, the *Pipeline Safety Act*, two of my amendments actually succeeded in committee to allow municipalities and First Nations to seek compensation from industry for damage caused by pipeline spills. Although this motion ceased to exist due to the prorogation of the House, an election and a new Parliament, the "convenience" for big parties of ensuring no smaller party or individual MP could move substantive amendments at report stage still proved too great for the new Liberal government.

When I read Dominic LeBlanc's mandate letter as government House leader, I was thrilled: "Respect for the opposition," "a spirit of generosity," no more improper use of prorogation or omnibus bills. In my first phone call with LeBlanc in November 2015, I asked if I could count on not having those dreaded motions crafted by the previous PMO brought back to apply to the committees of the upcoming 42nd sitting of Parliament. LeBlanc said he did not think I'd have anything to worry about.

Until I did. First one and then another Liberal committee chair approached me to ask how the rules worked to get my amendments in front of their committees. I managed to pull LeBlanc aside as he was leaving the House to ask if he had changed his mind. LeBlanc confirmed that the same motions were going to be passed in every committee. He tried to depersonalize it by claiming it was not directed at me and my rights, but rather to prevent the Bloc Québécois from slowing down the House. Within days, every committee was passing motions identical to the motion drafted under the Harper government. I literally ran from committee to committee to request the opportunity to argue against the motions. But nothing worked. All the Liberal MPs followed instructions and passed the motion. Many expressed personal regret to me afterward, but they felt they had to follow orders. None of the media noticed—or reported on this regression to Harper tactics.

The power of political parties is also exerted over the rights of free speech by members within a party. Although it is parliamentary tradition for the Speaker of the House to choose who is recognized in Question Period, over time and without any change in the rules, this authority has fallen to the party whip. It started innocently enough under Speaker Jeanne Sauvé. Speaker Sauvé said she could not see well enough to identify MPs from a distance. She asked the party whips if they would be so kind as to give her a list in advance of which MPs were to ask questions—and in what order. Unintentionally, more power was conferred to political parties. The convention was established that whips control who can ask questions. The Speaker now works from a list provided by the party whips that dictates both who will ask questions during Question Period and who will be making "members' statements," or "SO31s" (referring to Standing Order 31, which offers 60-second statements to members right before Question Period).

This was quickly extended to the control of which questions would be allowed to be asked. When I worked for the federal minister of environment in the Brian Mulroney years, questions and answers were not scripted. Over time, and certainly under the Harper regime, all parties engaged in a pathetic ritual called "QP prep." I found out about it when former finance minister Joe Oliver told me that he was not allowed to eat lunch on that particular day. "I have QP prep," he said in a fair impression of Eeyore at his most depressed. He was forced to practise his answers in front of PMO staff. To my shock, I learned that MPs in the opposition parties also had to practise questions in front of their spin doctors. No wonder it so often seems that MPs asking and answering questions do not even acknowledge what each other is saying—including asking the same question after it's been answered or providing the same non-answer to follow-up questions. They are simply sticking to a pre-approved script.

The control by the party whip over free speech has been directly challenged by at least one MP in recent years. Mark Warawa, the Conservative MP for Langley, had been on the party list to make a

60-second member's statement, but just before Question Period his whip told him he was not allowed to speak. On a point of order the next day, Warawa complained that his party had denied his freedom of speech:

> I was scheduled on March 20 [2013] from 2:00 to 2:15 to make an SO31. Fifteen minutes prior to that time, I was notified that my turn to present the SO31 had been removed. The reason I was given was that the topic was not approved of. However, there is no reason why an SO31 should be removed. The only person who can remove that is you, Mr. Speaker, according to SO31. The authority to remove an SO31 from any member of this House is solely in your hands, and the guiding is under SO31.[13]

Warawa's brave act was supported by eleven other Conservative MPs. I also stood to support his stand for free speech:

> For a specific case, may I say this is one of the most important points of privilege that I have heard in the brief almost two years I have been serving here. It cuts to the core of what is wrong with parliamentary democracy that the honourable government House leader could put before you a sports metaphor that we are here as teams, as brands or colours and we are all to take instructions from our team boss.
>
> We are not here as teams. The principle of Westminster parliamentary democracy is that we are here as representatives of our constituencies and our constituents. Incidentally, we are merely members of political parties. Political parties do not exist in our Constitution. They are not an essential part of our democracy. They have grown to be seen to be the most interesting thing going on and we have grown to see politics as some sort of sport. However, democracy is not a sport. We are not playing on teams, and each individual member has individual rights and the members for Langley

---

13. Aaron Wherry, "Mark Warawa Challenges the Soul of Our Parliamentary Democracy," *Maclean's*, 26 March 2013.

and Vegreville–Wainwright feel that their rights have been infringed upon.[14]

The Speaker chose not to rule directly on what had occurred, or on the practice of accepting lists from whips, but rather suggested that he would recognize individual MPs irrespective of the lists. "The right to seek the floor at any time is the right of each individual member of parliament and is not dependent on any other member of parliament," Speaker Scheer said. "If members want to be recognized, they will have to actively demonstrate that they wish to participate. They have to rise in their places and seek the floor."[15] Because Warawa had accepted the instructions from his whip and did not attempt to take the floor, the Speaker ruled he had not lost his right of free speech. Scheer said he would watch for those who tried to "catch his eye" and recognize those beyond the list from the whips. For the next few weeks I stood every day on every question to see if I could catch the Speaker's eye outside the pre-approved whip lists. Strangely, I never did.

Whips continue to control who speaks at every stage of parliamentary proceedings—speeches to bills, introduction of bills for first reading, members' statements and questions at Question Period. The rights and privileges of individual MPs and members of smaller parties have been slowly but steadily eroded. As noted, one of the key forces that has accomplished this is the growth of large and organized political parties; the other has been the growth of the PMO.

The Threat to Democracy That Is the Prime Minister's Office

Just as political parties are nowhere mentioned in our Constitution, neither is the Prime Minister's Office. In fact, there is scant reference to the prime minister at all. Canadians are so enveloped in US political culture that we often fail to observe these fundamental differences. In the US, there must be a vice-president constitutionally empowered to take the helm as president should the president die or become incapacitated. Of course, we have no such thing as a vice–prime minister. The prime minister is not our head of state. No constitutional imperative rests on any particular MP being the prime minister. In fact, it would not

---

14. Ibid.

15. Susan Delacourt, "Speaker Andrew Scheer's Ruling Yields Small Victory for MPs' Freedom of Speech," *Toronto Star*, 23 April 2013.

contravene the Constitution if, following an election, the House were to convene and elect a prime minister from among our ranks without regard to party standing. We could try to identify someone with the right skills—a good consensus-builder, an inspirational force.

Until the late 1960s, Canadian prime ministers did not consider the role a full-time job. From Sir John A. Macdonald to Lester B. Pearson, they all held some other cabinet portfolio as well as being prime minister. Until the Second World War, power was not concentrated in the cabinet. Parliament as a whole was paramount. But just as UK prime minister Sir Winston Churchill used the efficiency of cabinet to respond to wartime exigencies, so too did William Lyon Mackenzie King. For the first time in Canada's parliament, power became far more centralized in the cabinet. Between 1939 and 1945, cabinet passed over sixty thousand orders-in-council and over sixty thousand Treasury Board minutes. The volume of decision-making was simply beyond the capacity of Parliament to review. As political scientist Donald Savoie wrote, "The focus of activity and decision during the war had clearly shifted from parliament to cabinet and it would never shift back."[16]

True cabinet government meant that the role of the prime minister was essentially that of the chair of the meeting. Each minister had his responsibilities. Each minister was in charge of the department he headed, with the strong assistance of the professional, non-partisan civil service. The senior civil servant in each department, the deputy minister, played a key role in laying out policy options. The decision would be the minister's, but the expertise on which he or she drew came from a civil service that survived elections and provided something of policy consistency. There was a strong ethical construct of ministerial accountability. If a large error occurred within a minister's department, it was simply not acceptable to blame someone else. The minister would be expected to accept responsibility, and if the offence was of real significance, the minister was expected to resign.

The concentration of power having moved from Parliament to cabinet, the next big shift was in the creation of the Prime Minister's Office. Of course, the prime minister always had an office. Back in 1928 when future prime minister Pearson joined the civil service, he recalled that "the Prime Minister's Office, including stenographers, file clerks

---

16. Savoie, *Governing from the Centre*, 30.

and messengers, could not have comprised more than a dozen."[17] When Pearson was prime minister decades later, his principal secretary, Tom Kent, described it in much the same way. The office was larger, but the support staff for the prime minister were still of the clerical variety. Kent described Pearson's government as "Canada's last *cabinet* government. That, not prime ministerial autocracy, was how Canada's parliamentary democracy had worked for the first hundred years."[18]

It was when a charismatic new prime minister, Pierre Trudeau, looked at the resources and functioning of his office that he found it lacking. There was no central control over his ministers. With a keen awareness of the increasing role to be played by television and the news media, Trudeau wanted to coordinate activities—for example, to avoid ministers making major policy announcements on the same day. Trudeau laid the groundwork for the modern PMO. He hired bright, young Liberals and policy wonks and set about modernizing the prime minister's role. In effect, Trudeau invented the PMO.

The ministers used to true cabinet government were not impressed. Former prime minister John Turner has been a minister in both Pearson's and Trudeau's cabinets. One of the keen young staffers in Trudeau's PMO was Tom Axworthy, who went on to head the Queen's University Centre for the Study of Democracy in the School of Political Studies. Axworthy recalled being dispatched to ask Turner to consider a shift in the timing of some announcement and being rebuffed. Turner blasted him with instructions to go back to the prime minister and tell him he did not want to be told what to do "by the junior G-men of the PMO."[19] But over time, ministers became more amenable. In the Chrétien era, his right-hand man and chief of staff, Eddie Goldenberg, explained the benefits of having a strong PMO in managing media coverage: "Whether it is a good story or a bad story, there is no consistent story at all if you have more than two dozen cabinet ministers all

---

17. Ibid., 27.

18. Tom Kent, "Turner and Pearson: Cabinet and Trade," presentation to Politics with Purpose: Tribute to the Right Hon. John N. Turner, Centre for the Study of Democracy in the School of Political Studies, Queen's University, 24 October 2008.

19. Elizabeth McIninch and Arthur Milnes, eds., *Politics of Purpose: 40th Anniversary Edition* (Kingston: School of Policy Studies, 2009), viii.

making announcements any time they see fit, about anything they want without any planning or coordination."[20]

As each prime minister assumed power, each consolidated and expanded the powers of the prime minister they replaced. Mulroney's PMO was larger than Trudeau's; Chrétien's expanded once again. There was a brief pause and concern for the democratic deficit under Paul Martin. Through this period, as the power of the PMO grew, the role of the backbencher shrank. It was still the case that committee work gave the MPs in recognized parties an opportunity to make a real contribution. Through the Mulroney, Chrétien and Martin years, committees remained more respectful places where non-partisan work was still possible. A three-line whip, with which the governing party insists that all its MPs vote a certain way, would rarely be used to control the votes of backbench members. Such was the case when the Chrétien administration wished to keep the Liberal members of the Environment Committee from amending the proposed *Species at Risk Act* to make it an effective piece of legislation. But for the most part, individual MPs from the governing or opposition parties had an effective role on committees.

The scope for useful work for backbenchers was far reduced in Question Period. Whereas the role of MPs in responsible government is to hold the government to account, the rise of the PMO began to eradicate any such role. By the 1980s, MPs in the governing party who were not in cabinet were only allowed to ask fawning questions, drafted by the PMO with the goal of setting up the minister in question with an answer he or she could knock out of the park. Brent Rathgeber, a former Conservative MP who voluntarily moved to the status of independent, wrote extensively on the offensive nature of this practice in his book *Irresponsible Government*.[21]

The routine control of all statements by members of the governing party, through "talking points" scripted in the PMO, became the norm in the Chrétien years, although it was far from unknown under Mulroney. Still, as senior policy adviser to the minister of environment in that administration, I recall that statements by ministers were not scripted. My boss, Minister Tom McMillan, spoke off-the-cuff in Question

20. Eddie Goldenberg, *The Way It Works: Inside Ottawa* (Toronto: McClelland & Stewart, 2006), 78–79.

21. Rathgeber, *Irresponsible Government*, 69–71.

Period and never had to receive advance clearance for the speeches he delivered at conferences. The concentration of power as exercised over not only backbenchers but cabinet ministers hit its zenith under Harper. Senator Lowell Murray, former chief of staff to Mulroney, wrote a blistering critique of the control of ministers by the Harper PMO:

> The "Harper government's" trademark (literally) innovation has been to superimpose on this existing, centralized system a tightly run communications regime in which "message control" is the very essence of governance. Under this system, even strong ministers often become passengers on their own departmental ships, their destination and course set by remote control from Message Central at PCO/PMO. Parliament is not even in the picture. At its worst, the system makes ciphers of ministers, reducing from substantive to symbolic the autonomy, authority and accountability they should exercise.[22]

Don Martin wrote in his *National Post* column that Harper's ministers "play the role usually reserved for potted palms."[23]

The growth in the power of the PMO under Harper was deeply anti-democratic. Canadian constitutional conventions were violated one after the other. Prorogation was used to shut down the House to avoid a vote the prime minister knew he would lose. The power exerted by the PMO stretched into areas never before contaminated by direct political interference. Individual civil servants were told what to do. Lawyers in the Department of Justice were asked for legal advice but told "this is what we want you to say." Evidence was ignored or manufactured. Far from evidence-based policy-making, we had policy-based evidence-making. Scientists were silenced. Treaties were abrogated or adopted without a vote in the House. Our diplomats in foreign capitals were told no speeches could be given without advance PMO approval of every syllable. And Conservative senators were also placed under a stranglehold of communications.

---

22. Lowell Murray, "Harper Is Controlling, But Don't Think Trudeau or Mulcair Would Be Better," *Globe and Mail,* 11 September 2013.

23. Elizabeth May, "The Saga of Bill C-30: From Clean Air to Climate Change or Not," *Policy Options* (Institute for Research in Public Policy, May 2007).

Conclusion

Although there are some signs of change under the Justin Trudeau Liberals, the ongoing erosion of the rights of individual MPs continues. In 2008, a report of the Centre for the Study of Democracy at Queen's University concluded that Canada's parliament is "executive-centred, party-dominated [and] adversarial."[24] Even if the Trudeau government continues efforts to democratize Parliament, without legislated and rule-bound changes the characteristics of excessive party and PMO control remain a threat.

A series of laudatory reforms would include legislation requiring a vote to prorogue the House. In the normal course of traditional termination of a session, such a vote should easily carry with a super-majority of two-thirds. If ever again a prime minister is tempted to prorogue to avoid a confidence vote or political difficulty, the two-thirds requirement should suffice to preserve our constitutional principles of the supremacy of Parliament.

A key indicator of the degree of parliamentary democracy in Canada is the extent to which the rights of each and every MP are respected and equal. The single most important reform would be changing our voting system. A more consensus-based voting system, under some form of proportionality, will inevitably reduce the adversarial nature of Parliament. While not a panacea for all ills, consensus-based voting tends to enhance cross-party cooperation and reduce the excesses of prime ministerial power. So too would a change to ensure parliamentary seats reflect the way Canadians have actually voted. A more consensus-based decision-making method would reduce the power of the centre. If we as parliamentarians operated to ensure that all Canadians are treated equally, by ensuring that their representatives in Parliament are treated equally, the unhealthy trends of the past few decades could be reversed.

---

24. Thomas S. Axworthy, "Everything Old Is New Again: Observations on Parliamentary Reform," Centre for the Study of Democracy, Queen's University, April 2008.

How to Fix Question Period:
Ideas for Reform

Michael Cooper

Introduction

The practice of asking oral questions has existed throughout the history of parliamentary government in Canada. However, Question Period did not begin to gain prominence as the primary means for the opposition to hold government to account until 1956. Prior to then, Question Period had been primarily used to seek information from the government on sudden and unexpected events. Questions were not scheduled at any precise time of day; days would often pass without a single question being posed. This changed when the Liberal government of Louis St. Laurent sought to limit debate on the construction of a pipeline from western to central Canada. The Conservatives, led by John Diefenbaker, turned to Question Period as a forum for expressing opposition to the pipeline. By 1958 the Liberals, who found themselves in opposition, turned the tables on the new Prime Minister Diefenbaker by using Question Period as the main forum in which to critique the Conservative government. Question Period had become a daily event in the House of Commons, with an increasingly dramatic tone, and it became closely followed by the media.[25]

---

25. Peter C. Dobell and John Reid, "A Larger Role for the House of Commons, Part I: Question Period," *Parliamentary Government* 40 (April 1992), 6.

Today Question Period is the most-watched, most-scrutinized activity in the House of Commons. Lasting only forty-five minutes of a typical eight-and-a-half-hour day of Parliament sitting, it is usually the only time that most MPs are present in the Chamber, the public galleries are filled to capacity with spectators, and the attention of members of the press gallery is intensely focused on the goings-on inside the Chamber. The first several minutes of Question Period are broadcast live by national cable news networks and on many AM radio stations across Canada. Sound bites from this forty-five-minute daily ritual are played on news broadcasts and quoted in daily news reports. Question Period is what most Canadians think of when they think about what goes on in the House of Commons. As veteran MP Brian Tobin wrote in his memoir *All in Good Time*:

> I was mentioned in dozens of media stories detailing the activities of Question Period, but only once in reference to my committee work...So 13 years of committee work yielded one mention in a *Globe and Mail* column written by Hugh Winsor, while 13 minutes of give-and-take in Question Period could earn headlines and evening TV news coverage day after day. That kind of sums it up.[26]

Question Period serves as an important accountability tool. It is a forum where MPs from across the political spectrum can question the government on issues of public importance and ensure that the executive is held accountable for its actions.[27] However, is Question Period in its present format actually working? Many parliamentarians, academics, members of the media and Canadians at large would answer no to this question. The level of decorum in the House during Question Period is often said to be wanting. Questions and answers are scripted and are said to lack substance. There is a lack of spontaneity. Backbench members of the government and opposition are largely excluded from the opportunity to participate.

All these criticisms of Question Period have some merit. I don't believe Question Period is broken. However, it isn't perfect either. Many

---

26. Brian Tobin, *All in Good Time* (Toronto: Penguin Canada, 2002): 60–61.

27. Frances H. Ryan, "Can Question Period Be Reformed?," *Canadian Parliamentary Review* (Autumn 2009), 18.

of the oft-cited criticisms of Question Period today can be fixed with a few relatively minor changes that I will set out in this chapter. They include the following:

- *The Speaker needs to exercise authority*—Decorum can be improved if the Speaker vigorously and consistently enforces existing rules. In particular, naming and shaming members who behave badly and expelling persistent offenders would have a positive impact. But the Speaker can't do it alone. He or she must also work with the House leaders and whips of all parties to elevate the level of decorum. Only when all parties are onside in addressing the issue of decorum will significant headway be made toward improving the tone of the House during Question Period.

- *Re-evaluate the 35-second rule for questions and answers*—Question Period could become more substantive by allowing for longer questions and answers. The current 35-second allotment doesn't cut it. More substance would also help improve the tone and level of decorum in the House.

- *Put an end to clapping*—Clapping in recent years has become excessive. It causes disruption, lessens decorum in the House and wastes a lot of time. Putting an end to clapping would save a lot of time and help improve the level of decorum of Question Period. Also, if members could actually hear the questions being asked and the answers being provided, this might also elevate the substance of Question Period.

- *Restrict the use of lists*—Opposition parties control lines of questioning by imposing lists of which members will question the government in what order. Lists have made it difficult for backbench government and opposition MPs alike to participate. Restricting lists to the first thirty minutes of Question Period would give the opposition plenty of time to coordinate questioning on key issues of the day, leaving fifteen minutes for other MPs to participate.

■ *Special Question Periods*—The introduction of special Question Periods, such as a biweekly Prime Minister's Question Period or one specifically devoted to a major issue of the day, could complement the existing Question Period format by providing opportunities for members to drill down in detail on issues of public importance.

Problems with Question Period and Attempts at Reform

The official purpose of Question Period is "to seek information from the government and to call it to account for its actions."[28] On many days, this purpose is not readily apparent. To watch Question Period is to see tightly scripted rhetorical questions from the opposition; puffball questions from government members; ministers providing answers to questions by reading directly from talking points; constant clapping; routine standing ovations in response to less-than-riveting questions and answers; and plenty of heckling, occasional desk-banging and other rowdy behaviour that would not be tolerated anywhere else in Canada (except in provincial legislatures).

In the media age that we live in, a quiet Question Period may be good for the government, not necessarily for the opposition. In this context, Jay Hill made these observations about the unsuccessful efforts of the fifty-two Reform MPs elected in 1993, of which he was one, to improve the level of decorum during Question Period:

> With fifty-two seats, two shy of forming the official opposition at the time, the Reform Party came to Ottawa looking to change the way politics was done—including Question Period. For the first few months of the 35th parliament in 1994 we asked probing, thoughtful and respectful questions, sat in silence during the answers, and only occasionally

28. Andrea Ulrich, "A Question of Accountability: Is Question Period in Canada Working?," *Queen's Policy Review* 2, no. 2 (Fall 2011), 2.

applauded one of our questioners, usually our leader Preston Manning...the media constantly derided us as "ineffective" and "naïve." Even our supporters began to question when they did not see us on the nightly news. We soon found out that in the House of Commons, like in many other places of work, it is inevitable that people bring themselves and their behaviour down to the lowest common denominator.[29]

Toward the end of the spring 2016 sitting, Liberal government MPs started to refrain from clapping; they were not as diligent in refraining from heckling. While I believe that less clapping during Question Period is a good thing, I have no reason to believe that the Liberals' new approach to clapping is a virtuous effort rather than a self-interested strategy to calm Question Period criticism of their government. It was not long ago that many of the same Liberal MPs, while in opposition, engaged in their fair share of Question Period rowdiness.

I do not count myself among those who want to see an end to all forms of heckling and other forms of boisterous behaviour that members have long engaged in during Question Period. Quite simply, Question Period is not an afternoon tea party. And I don't believe that it would be improved if it turned into one. That said, I do believe that decorum could be improved. Not all forms of heckling are helpful. Likewise, highly scripted questions and answers and general grandstanding sometimes make Question Period appear like a time when MPs play the role of C-rate actors for forty-five minutes instead of duly elected representatives of their constituents.

The introduction of television cameras in 1977 fostered many of the objectionable features of Question Period as MPs from all sides of the House began to "play for the cameras." After the 1984 election, decorum during Question Period arguably reached an all-time low. In that year's election, Brian Mulroney's Tories won a historic 211 of 282 seats in the House of Commons. The Liberals fell to their worst showing ever with a mere forty seats. The opposition Liberals, led by the infamous, self-described "Rat Pack," compensated for the small share of seats they held by filling Question Period with attention-grabbing, over-the-top

---

29. Jay Hill, "Reflections on Reforming Question Period," *Canadian Parliamentary Review* (Winter 2010), 4.

questions, members often yelling at the top of their lungs.[30] While the Liberal Party benefited from plenty of publicity about the disorderly antics of its members, Canadians' impression of Question Period and of Parliament as a whole was diminished.

In 1991, the Citizens' Forum on Canada's Future, commissioned by the Mulroney government to consult Canadians in the lead-up to the Charlottetown Accord, received a strong message from Canadians that they had lost faith in the political process and in Parliament.[31] The commissioners reflected the strength of these sentiments by including, as one of their most strongly stated recommendations, "a careful review of the Question Period and how it is organized, with an eye on the more productive Question Periods in other parliamentary systems."[32] The commissioners further observed that Canadians had become concerned that Parliament was "too partisan" and that "the abrasive character of adversarial debate in the House of Commons, particularly in Question Period," had "undermined parliamentary decorum and the public's confidence in parliamentary institutions."[33]

In 1993, the House of Commons Standing Committee on House Management undertook a study on parliamentary reform. In its report, the committee provided a critical assessment of Question Period, observing that Canadians find "shenanigans" that accompany Question Period "immature" and "unproductive."[34] The Committee recommended significant changes, including 1) allowing more questions by reducing the amount of time for questions and answers, 2) restrictions on the use of lists, and 3) a roster system for ministers.[35]

Fourteen years later, the Canadian public's perception of Question Period appeared not to have changed for the better. In 2007, the Harper government commissioned a research report entitled *Public Consultations on Canada's Democratic Institutions and Practices* with a

---

30. Keith Beardsley, "Smug promises won't improve Question Period behaviour," *National Post*, 27 May 27 2011, http://news.nationalpost.com/full-comment/keith-beardsley-smug-promises-wont-improve-question-period-behaviour.

31. Standing Committee on House Management, "Eighty-First Report" (House of Commons, April 1, 1993), 7.

32. Dobell and Reid, "A Larger Role for the House of Commons," 5.

33. Standing Committee on House Management, "Eighty-First Report," 7–8.

34. Ibid., 15.

35. Ibid., 15–17.

mandate to canvass the public's views on the functioning of our democratic institutions.[36] The report found:

> Some forum participants felt strongly that the open debate of QP is essential to democracy. On the other hand, quite a number of participants called for more decorum, substance, and to some extent cooperation among Members speaking in QP.[37]

In 2010, my colleague, MP Michael Chong, introduced a motion calling on the Standing Committee on Procedure and House Affairs to study recommended changes to the rules governing Question Period. These included 1) elevating decorum and strengthening the use of discipline by the Speaker, 2) lengthening the time for questions and answers, 3) requiring ministers to respond to questions asked of them, 4) allocating half of the questions each day to backbench members, 5) dedicating Wednesday to questions to the prime minister, and 6) dedicating the rest of the week to questions to ministers other than the prime minister.[38]

At the time, Chong said that he was motivated to introduce the motion because Canadians had become disappointed in the level of decorum in the House of Commons, particularly during Question Period. As Chong said:

> Teachers have told me that the level of behaviour in question period is such that they will not take their classes here anymore. This is the surest sign that question period needs to be reformed…Question period has become a time where behaviour that is not permitted in any boardroom, dining room, or classroom regularly occurs here in the people's room.[39]

---

36. Frances H. Ryan, "The Ineffectiveness of Question Period," Canadian Study of Parliament Group, national essay competition winner, winter 2008, 5.

37. Ibid.

38. Canada, *House of Commons Debates*. 40th Parliament, 3rd session, Hansard 050, May 27, 2010, http://www.parl.gc.ca/HousePublications/Publication.aspx?Language=E&Mode=1&Parl=40&Ses=3&DocId=4559699

39. Michael Chong, "What to Do About Question Period: A Roundtable," *Canadian Parliamentary Review* (Autumn 2010), 2.

The motion received wide support in the House, passing in a vote of 235 to 44. Following its passage, the Procedure and House Affairs committee began to study changes to Question Period. However, it did not complete its work before the May 2011 federal election, and the motion died with the dissolution of Parliament.[40]

While Chong's motion may have died, the issue of reforming Question Period has not. In the 2015 election, the Liberal Party platform included a commitment to "reform Question Period so that all members, including the prime minister, are held to greater account."[41] The Liberal platform included a commitment to introduce a Prime Minister's Question Period "to improve that level of direct accountability; empower the Speaker to sanction members; allow more time for questions and answers; and explore ways to make Question Period more relevant, including through the use of online technologies."[42] Since winning the election, the Liberals have yet to implement any of these commitments.

Decorum

Lack of decorum is probably the most commonly criticized aspect of today's Question Period. Anyone who watches it for five minutes can see why. Questions and answers are routinely interrupted by heckling. Enlightened chants of "Shame!" and "Time!" are par for the course. There is no shortage of rowdy applause—sometimes interrupting members asking or answering questions—besides occasional desk-banging. Due to the noise it is often difficult to hear the questions asked or answers provided.

For many new members to the House, their first Question Periods can be shocking. Glen Pearson, the former Liberal MP for London North Centre, wrote that when he attended his first Question Period as a member of Parliament he felt like he had been "swallowed by a hornet's nest."[43] Liberal MP Frank Baylis described his first Question Period experiences this way:

---

40. Michael Chong, "Yes, We Can Fix Question Period. We Already Know How," *iPolitics*, January 22, 2016, http://ipolitics.ca/2016/01/22/yes-we-can-fix-question-period-we-already-know-how/.

41. Liberal Party of Canada, "Question Period," https://www.liberal.ca/realchange/question-period/.

42. Ibid.

43. Glen Pearson, "Some Personal Thoughts on Question Period," *Canadian Parliamentary Review* (Winter 2010), 2.

When I arrived here, I was so shocked by this bad behaviour that I would sidle up to one MP after another and ask what they thought about Question Period, and I would get two responses. If it were a new MP like me, the answer would be, "Oh, my gosh, it's incredible. It's unacceptable and I can't believe I'm in this environment." If I sidled up to someone else who had been here a long time, the person would say, "Oh, Frank, it's not so bad." They had become acclimatized. Human beings are capable of becoming acclimatized.[44]

I have to admit that I was not surprised by what I saw during my first Question Period experiences. Before I was elected, I had long been a Question Period consumer. I started tuning in when I was in Grade 6 and have tuned in ever since. Twenty years of viewing Question Period on TV made me "acclimatized" to the rough-and-tumble atmosphere by the time I took my seat as an MP. Instead of being shocked, as many members genuinely are, I was ready to partake in the back and forth. Over time my heckling has diminished, though I occasionally contribute. I've toned it down partially because as Question Period has grown routine, the novelty of it all has worn thin.

The House of Commons can be a rowdy place, and there is good reason for it to be. After all, it is a place where some of the biggest and most contentious issues facing Canada are debated. There are often sharp differences of opinion among members, who collectively cover the mainstream Canadian political spectrum. Those differences are regularly debated with passion by members. In this context, it is easy to see how an activity such as Question Period can get heated.

Nonetheless, it is fair to say that the level of decorum in the House generally and in Question Period particularly has dropped over the years. I am not sure that the level of decorum today is any different than it was ten years ago. However, I am certain that the level of decorum has declined from where it was twenty years ago, when I first started to watch House proceedings. Indeed, while the issue of decorum is often one of the first things thought of when the topic of Question Period

---

44. Canada, *House of Commons Debates*. 42nd Parliament, 1st session, Hansard 089, October 6, 2016, http://www.parl.gc.ca/HousePublications/Publication.aspx?Language=E&Mode=1&Parl=42&Ses=1&DocId=8485068

arises, it is not even mentioned in former Speaker Peter Milliken's 1968 bachelor's thesis, "Question Period: Developments from 1960 to 1967."

So what can be done to improve decorum? I believe three things would go a long way toward improving it. First, the Speaker needs to exercise his or her authority by being more proactive in calling out members who routinely behave badly. Second, the current format of 35-second questions and answers needs to be re-evaluated. Third, clapping should be banned. These changes, taken together, will not only improve the overall level of decorum, they will also help return substance and spontaneity to Question Period.

The Speaker and the Need to Exercise Authority

One of the most obvious ways for decorum to improve during Question Period is for the Speaker to exercise the considerable authority given to him or her in presiding over House proceedings. The Speaker has the implicit authority to rule any question as out of order if satisfied that the question is in contravention of House rules, including lacking decorum. The Speaker may refuse to recognize a member. The Speaker may shut down Question Period early for the day by eliminating question slots. The Speaker may call out members. And most significantly, the Speaker may name a member and have him or her removed from the House for the day.[45]

In recent years, Speakers have tended to shy away from intervening, allowing members to self-regulate Question Period. That was not always the case. For example, when Marcel Lambert was chosen as Speaker in 1962, he maintained that the primary purpose of Question Period was "to elicit important information urgently."[46] To further this, Lambert ruled many questions out of order, including driving questions that were not aimed at eliciting important, urgent information from the government to the order paper. During his short tenure, Speaker Lambert ruled an average of 22.2 percent of questions out of order.[47] Lambert's successor, Alan Macnaughton, took a much more relaxed approach to the House, ruling just 2.4 percent of questions out of order in 1963. In

---

45. Audrey O'Brien and Marc Bosc, *House of Commons Procedure and Practice,* 2nd ed. (Ottawa: House of Commons, 2009), 496.

46. Peter Milliken, "Question Period: Developments from 1960 to 1967" (bachelor's thesis, Queen's University, March 31, 1968), 14.

47. Ibid., 13.

the 1964–65 and 1965 sessions, Speaker Macnaughton ruled 7.4 percent and 6.1 percent of questions out of order. However Lucien Lamoureux, who succeeded Macnaughton, took a similar approach to Lambert, strictly exercising his authority over the House and ruling 20.9 percent of questions out of order in 1966–67.[48]

It should be noted that the decorum of the House was not a major issue at the time. Lambert's routine daily interventions were directed at seeing that Question Period fulfilled the purpose of seeking questions on important and urgent matters of government. Lamoureux's interventions were motivated by his desire to see a shorter Question Period where questions and answers were delivered in rapid-fire succession.[49] Nonetheless, the foregoing illustrates the degree to which previous Speakers exercised their authority over Question Period. A Speaker who exercised his or her authority with the same vigour and consistency as former Speakers Lambert and Lamoureux directed at badly behaved members would almost certainly have a significant and immediate effect on improving the level of decorum during Question Period.

The modern approach taken by Speakers to more or less allow members to self-regulate Question Period started when James Jerome became Speaker. After 1975, Question Period became an increasingly open forum where all manner of questions were allowed to be asked, notwithstanding some of the guidelines that had been developed and the urgency requirement in the standing order.[50] After the Liberal Rat Pack arrived on Parliament Hill, Speaker John Bosley tried to assert authority in an effort to restore order to a restive House of Commons. This included routinely expelling rowdy members for the sitting day.[51] In 1986 Bosley, in setting forth guidelines for conduct during Question Period, reminded members that "the public in large numbers do watch, and the House, recognizing Question Period is often an intense time, should be on its best possible behaviour."[52]

Since Bosley, every successive Speaker has faced the same challenge of presiding over an often unruly House during Question

---

48. Ibid., 13.
49. Ibid., 20.
50. O'Brien and Bosc, *House of Commons Procedure and Practice*, 495.
51. Ibid., 496.
52. Statement by Speaker John Bosley, "Speaker's Ruling," *Canadian Parliamentary Review* (Summer 1986), 42.

Period. In his aforementioned 1986 ruling establishing guidelines for Question Period, Bosley recognized that it would be "practically impossible" to bring back the "old rules," where questions outside the scope of seeking important information from the government could be ruled out of order, and questions of a non-urgent nature could be pushed to the order paper.[53]

I believe that open, back-and-forth exchanges with minimal intervention from the Speaker are important to maintain. The ability of the opposition to use Question Period as a forum for holding the government accountable would be significantly curtailed if questions were ruled out of order, as they once were, for questioning a minister about matters reported in the media or statements made outside of the House.[54] The Speaker can help improve the tone and level of decorum of the House during Question Period less by enforcing rules around content and more by directing attention to members who bring disorder to the House. That includes calling individual members out and removing repeat offenders from the House for the day. To effectively change the behaviour of members, this practice must be carried out as a matter of course. Also, importantly, the Speaker must work collaboratively with the House leaders and whips to improve decorum. Unless they also face internal consequences, members may not be dissuaded by the Speaker's rulings from engaging in poor behaviour.

When he assumed the Speaker's chair in the 42nd Parliament, Geoff Regan made a point of calling out individual members. During the spring 2016 sitting, he named individual members on twenty-five occasions.[55] I believe that this action alone has helped to improve the level of decorum, or at least discouraged it from getting worse. I was in fact one of the first members called out by Regan. I had become fairly animated during an answer provided by François-Philippe Champagne, the parliamentary secretary to the minister of finance. At the conclusion of Champagne's answer, Regan gently admonished me that as "a new member, there are some things not to learn from older members...

53. Ibid.
54. Ibid.
55. Éric Grenier, "Naming and Shaming Hecklers in the House of Commons," CBC News, September 19, 2016, http://www.cbc.ca/news/politics/grenier-hecklers-regan-commons-1.3636482.

and one of them is heckling."[56] Being called out by the Speaker certainly caused me to refrain from heckling for the rest of that Question Period, and it has since made me more judicious in my interventions.

There is a perception by many of my Conservative colleagues that Speaker Regan has a tendency to single out opposition members, particularly Conservatives. Conservative members were called out on twenty of the twenty-five occasions in which Speaker Regan named a member. NDP members were named on three of the twenty-five occasions. Only twice were Liberal members called out.[57] Overall, I found that Speaker Regan did a good job in his first year in exercising his authority to encourage better decorum. He has my full respect and support in his efforts.

The 35-Second Format for Questions and Answers

Questions and answers in Question Period are limited to thirty-five seconds each. The 35-second rule has been in place since the 1997 election. That election produced what has been characterized as "pizza pie" Parliament, with five political parties (Liberal, Reform, Bloc Québécois, New Democrat and Progressive Conservative) having official party status. After the election, Speaker Gilbert Parent met with the House leaders of the five parties and reached an agreement with them to reduce the time for questions and answers to thirty-five seconds to accommodate the participation of all five parties. Prior to 1997, questions and answers were allowed to be longer, at the Speaker's discretion.[58]

There is merit to keeping questions and answers short. Shorter questions and answers allows for more questions and therefore more participation from members and more efficient use of time. Former Speaker Lucien Lamoureux opined, "If you have long questions and long answers, interest is lost and it becomes meaningless."[59] In a 1993 report, the Standing Committee on House Management recommended reducing the length of questions and answers, observing, "Members are supposed to ask questions, rather than deliver speeches. By the

---

56. Canada, *House of Commons Debates*. 42nd Parliament, 1st session, Hansard 009, January 26, 2016, http://www.parl.gc.ca/HousePublications/Publication.aspx?Language=E&Mode=1&Parl=42&Ses=1&DocId=8073490
57. Ibid.
58. Chong, "Yes, We Can Fix Question Period."
59. Milliken, "Question Period," 20.

same token, the answers of ministers should be brief, and relevant."[60] Unfortunately, since the introduction of the 35-second rule, we have not seen crisper, more-to-the-point questions from members or more direct and relevant responses from ministers. Rather, the 35-second rule has discouraged substantive exchanges in favour of rhetorical questions and answers.

Allowing longer questions and answers does not necessarily solve the issue of rhetorical questions and answers, which were also common-place before the introduction of the 35-second rule. However, the extension of the time limit would at least allow the opportunity for more substantive questions and answers (such things can rarely be condensed into thirty-five seconds). Most 35-second questions and answers are reduced to one or two sound bites. There is no opportunity for a member to provide context or to dig deep on any topic. Often, only the surface is scratched; simplicity over substance is encouraged.

In a 1995 study of parliamentary questioning in western European parliaments, Matti Wiberg agrees that longer time allotments allow for more substantive answers. Wiberg noted that shorter answers might serve the political purpose of a questioner who is motivated to embar-rass "[a] minister's lack of competence and of relevant information" but that "[a] rapid answer is not always the most informative in adminis-trative terms."[61] Longer questions and answers might also encourage greater spontaneity. Thirty-five-second questions and answers leave very little room for error. Even a slight slip-up is enough to ruin the effec-tiveness of a 35-second question or answer. As a result, most members posing questions read strictly from prescreened notes. Likewise, minis-ters often read word for word from prepared talking points. Longer questions and answers might require members asking questions and ministers answering them to rely less on their notes and to think more on their feet.

Clapping

My colleague Michael Chong observed that "In the history of parlia-mentary democracy, our present House of Commons must be full of

---

60. Standing Committee on House Management, "Eighty-First Report," 16.

61. Matti Wiberg, "Parliamentary Questioning: Control by Communication?" in *Parliaments and Majority Rule in Western Europe*, ed. Herbert Döring (New York: St. Martin's Press, 1995), 199.

exceptional orators[,] for virtually all questions and answers are followed by clapping and standing ovations."[62] Journalist Aaron Wherry tallied eighty-five rounds of applause, twenty-four of which were either full or partial standing ovations, during a single routine sitting in January 2016.[63] Clapping in the House of Commons has become a reflexive habit of MPs. Often when opposition leaders are recognized by the Speaker to commence a round of questions, they are met with a standing ovation by their caucus members before they have spoken a word. Many of the questions in the leaders' rounds, too, are similarly met with standing ovations, which continue throughout Question Period. Often members don't know what they are clapping for, but do so because others around them are.

I admit that I am guilty of this. I don't always listen to every question or answer in Question Period, and I occasionally find myself standing with the rest of my colleagues, giving a standing ovation to a question that I did not even hear. Any member who is being honest will admit to doing the same. Frankly, it doesn't feel right to sit in your chair while everyone around you is on their feet. And the optics aren't great either, especially if you are on-camera.

Clapping was once banned from the House of Commons. Members expressed their approval by desk-thumping—a practice that is continued in some provincial legislatures. However, with the introduction of television, it was thought that clapping was visually preferable to the traditional desk-thumping. Most provincial legislatures followed suit around the same time, for the same reason. Over the years, clapping seems to have consumed more time in Question Period. Clapping has evolved into more and more standing ovations. Twenty years ago when I started to watch Question Period, standing ovations were rare. Today, there are probably on average a dozen standing ovations during a single Question Period.

What is the problem with clapping? After all, clapping to show appreciation or approval is as old as civilization itself. It is a natural human reaction that signals approval. The problem is that it is taking

---

62. Michael Chong, "Rethinking Question Period and Debate in the House of Commons," *Canadian Parliamentary Review* (Autumn 2008), 6.

63. Aaron Wherry, "To Reform Parliament, MPs Might Start by Holding Their Applause," CBC News, January 29, 2016, http://www.cbc.ca/news/politics/applause-question-period-wherry-1.3422691.

up a lot of time. Vicki Huntington, a British Columbia MLA, estimates that as much as twenty minutes per week is taken up by clapping during Question Period in the BC legislature.[64] Twenty minutes would be a conservative estimate for the House of Commons. This time would allow for additional questions or longer questions and answers.

Also, clapping has lost any meaning, since nearly every question, no matter how standard or generic, is applauded. Moreover, the constant rounds of applause and standing ovations create a significant amount of noise. As a result, like heckling, they contribute to making questions and answers difficult to hear. Members would start listening more attentively to questions and answers if the clapping stopped, if for no other reason than it would be a lot easier to hear what was being said.

Clapping is not permitted in the mother of parliaments—the UK House of Commons. So rare is clapping there that last year it was described as an "extraordinary scene" when new Scottish National MPs broke into applause in support of their leader. They were sternly reminded by the Speaker "to show some respect for the traditions of this Chamber," including "the convention that we do not clap in this Chamber."[65] A House of Commons modernization committee set up by Tony Blair's government in 1998 said new MPs found it "incomprehensible" that they could not applaud at the end of a speech, as is commonplace at other gatherings.[66] However, the committee recommended maintaining the clapping ban, noting:

> While we agree that spontaneous clapping at the end of a speech could in no way be interpreted as disturbance of the speaker, there is a danger that such a practice might be open to abuse and could lead in certain circumstances to orchestration of what would amount to standing ovations with the success or failure of a speech being judged not by its content but by the relative length of the ovation at the end.[67]

64. Dirk Meissner, "Bid to Ban Applause in B.C. Legislature Rejected with Rousing Ovation," CBC News, May 14, 2016, http://www.cbc.ca/news/canada/british-columbia/bc-legislature-applause-ban-1.3582740.

65. Brian Wheeler, "Why Are MPs Banned From Clapping?," BBC News, May 28, 2015, http://www.bbc.com/news/uk-politics-32913113.

66. Ibid.

67. Ibid.

The Canadian House of Commons is a real-life example of what the committee feared would happen if clapping were allowed in Britain's House of Commons.

Closer to home, Quebec's National Assembly voted unanimously in September 2015 to ban clapping during Question Period.[68] At least initially, the ban had a significant impact in toning down the temperature of the Chamber during Question Period. The Speaker of the National Assembly, Jacques Chagnon, noted that more questions than usual were asked in the first non-clapping Question Period, due to time saved.[69] While the previous level of noise returned to the National Assembly, there are no plans to reverse the no-clapping rule during Question Period. Overall, it appears that the no-clapping rule has had a small but positive impact on the level of decorum in the National Assembly. It is time for the House of Commons to take its cue from Quebec's National Assembly and Britain's House of Commons by putting an end to clapping during Question Period.

Use of Lists

In 1975, Speaker James Jerome established that asking oral questions was a right, not a privilege, of members.[70] Ironically, around this time Question Period lists were introduced, which has restricted the ability of members to ask questions. Under the list system, the whips and House leaders of each party present the Speaker with a list of members to recognize during Question Period. Prior to the introduction of Question Period lists, members who wished to ask questions would rise to catch the eye of the Speaker. The Speaker had the ability to decide who to recognize. Question Time in the UK continues to operate in this fashion.

In the early 1970s, lists were introduced as a means of managing coordinated attacks by the opposition on the government. Originally, only the names of the first few questioners were put on lists.[71] There was still opportunity for members to rise if they wanted to ask a question but were not on the list. Lists expanded after 1977 with the introduction

---

68. Les Perreaux, "Striking Silence Descends on Quebec's Question Period After Peace Pact," *Globe and Mail*, September 18, 2015, http://www.theglobeandmail.com/news/national/striking-silence-descends-on-quebecs-question-period-after-peace-pact/article26442456/.

69. Ibid.

70. O'Brien and Bosc, *House of Commons Procedure and Practice*, 495.

71. Standing Committee on House Management, "Eighty-First Report," 17.

of television cameras. Before cameras, it was not an issue when the Speaker would have to spend ten or twenty seconds looking at the seating chart to be reminded of the name of an honourable member's riding. However, this "dead air" became a problem with the introduction of cameras. Hence, there began to be a further reliance on lists to aid the Speaker.[72] By the 1990s, almost all questions in Question Period came from parties' respective daily lists.

Lists have negatively affected Question Period in at least two ways. First, Question Period has become a highly orchestrated event. Every question is scripted in advance and vetted through the House leaders' offices. Second, lists make it difficult for backbench MPs to participate in Question Period. There are only a handful of slots on the daily list for government backbenchers to ask questions. As a result, most are all but shut out of Question Period. It is not unheard of for backbench government MPs to go through the entire term without asking a single question in Question Period. While most question slots on the daily list are reserved for the opposition, it isn't much easier for opposition back-benchers to participate, because most questions are reserved for MPs designated as critics or deputy critics.

Upon being elected, I was fortunate to be named the Conservative deputy justice critic. As a result, our Question Period team routinely taps me to ask questions on justice issues. Likewise, I often submit questions on justice issues on my own initiative and have been gener-ally successful in getting them approved. However, I have found it more difficult to get on the Question Period rotation when I wish to ask ques-tions about issues outside of my justice critic portfolio. It is even more difficult for members who are not critics or deputy critics to make it into the Question Period rotation.

I have found our Conservative Question Period team great to work with and supportive of all members of the caucus. However, every morning these staffers have the task of identifying the issues that we as Conservatives want to highlight for the day. The appropriate critics and deputy critics are inevitably tapped to prepare questions on those issues. With only so many slots, it's difficult to include other MPs in the daily Question Period rotation.

---

72. Chong, "Yes, We Can Fix Question Period."

Calls to restrict the use of lists have been longstanding. For example, the Standing Committee on House Management recommended the restriction of lists in a 1993 report, noting that it would make Question Period less orchestrated. The committee also observed that a restriction on lists would strengthen the Speaker's hand. Members who engage in vitriolic behaviour or ignore the Speaker's warnings might not be recognized during Question Period by the Speaker. In this way, a restriction on the use of lists might be an incentive for members to behave better and could increase civility in the House.[73]

I do not favour doing away with lists entirely. Coordination is required for the opposition to effectively use Question Period as a forum for raising issues and holding the government to account. Lists serve that purpose, in that they make it easier for the opposition to do its job. However, this has come with the loss of spontaneity and the ability of many members to ask questions, which as noted is not a privilege but a right of members.

I recommend restricting lists during the last fifteen minutes of Question Period. During this time any member, whether on the government or opposition side, could rise to be recognized by the Speaker. Designating the last fifteen minutes of Question Period in this way would inject some spontaneity back into Question Period and provide an opportunity for backbench government and opposition MPs to participate while maintaining the ability of opposition parties to coordinate their daily critique of the government.

Special Question Periods

A roster system, whereby ministers would answer questions in Question Period on a rotating basis, would allow opposition members time to prepare detailed questions and would encourage a greater policy focus. In this regard, a roster system could make Question Period more substantive. Former Speaker Peter Milliken advocated for a roster system in his 1968 thesis. So did the Standing Committee on House Management in 1993. More recently, MP Michael Chong lent his voice in support.[74] In the 2015 election, the Liberal Party endorsed the idea of a kind of roster system for the prime minister with the introduction of a Westminster-style weekly Prime Minister's Question Period.

---

73. Standing Committee on House Management, "Eighty-First Report," 17.
74. Ryan, "The Ineffectiveness of Question Period," 10.

Proponents of a roster system have argued that with the mandatory attendance of the prime minister and ministers under our current Question Period, questions are not as focused as they could be because they can be directed at anyone and are frequently aimed at the prime minister.[75] A roster system would encourage a more efficient use of time for ministers and their staffs. Michael Chong observed that when he was in cabinet he spent on average "an hour or more of preparation, an hour of Question Period itself and an hour of analyzing what just happened in Question Period."[76] He observed, "These three hours a day out of a minister's schedule, every day, five days a week, takes much time away from the important work of running a portfolio. This is not productive time as, most often, many ministers do not answer a single question in Question Period."[77]

While these are strong arguments, I have some concerns that give me pause. A roster system might encourage more policy-focused Question Periods and save ministers plenty of time; however, such a system would also likely lessen the ability of the opposition to hold the government accountable. Question Period is relevant to the media and of interest to the public when the matters raised are topical. In the present seven-days-a-week, twenty-four-hour news cycle, the lifespan of an issue is short, with public interest quickly shifting to some other topic. When an issue arises in a minister's department that is of public interest, the current Question Period format provides the opportunity to raise that issue while it is still on the public radar. Additionally, a roster system would not improve the spontaneity of Question Period.

Nonetheless, there may be some merit to experimenting with the roster system while leaving the current format of Question Period, with mandatory attendance, intact. In this regard, consideration could be given to designating one Question Period every two weeks to questions directed exclusively to the prime minister. A weekly Prime Minister's Question Period would likely result in the prime minister only attending that Question Period, once a week. I believe there is value in the prime minister attending more often. The current format provides the opposition with the opportunity to ask questions of the prime minister on topics of the day—not topics that are two or three days old. A biweekly

75. Ryan, "Can Question Period Be Reformed?," 20.
76. Chong, "Rethinking Question Period and Debate, 6.
77. Ibid.

Prime Minister's Question Period might provide members the opportunity to engage with the prime minister on a more substantive basis while preserving the ability of members to ask questions of the prime minister on a more routine basis.

Likewise, there may be some benefit in holding occasional special Question Periods with a specific minister on a major topic of the day. In 1990 the House approved a special motion permitting a concentrated debate on the Mulroney government's GST legislation. Following statements from the minister of finance and one speaker from each opposition party, the minister of finance took questions for an hour, based on the Question Period format.[78] The event was "judged as a great success by all the parties as well as by the media" and "was well reported."[79] Holding special Question Period sessions focused on major issues would allow for substantive questions and answers. Such occasional, issues-based Question Periods would likely draw media interest because they would be outside of the routine and on major issues of interest to the public.

Conclusion

Reforming Question Period is not a new topic. As far back as 1963, Speaker Alan Macnaughton tried to reduce the length of Question Period.[80] In 1993, the Standing Committee on House Management recommended significant changes to it. In 2010, the House of Commons voted overwhelmingly in favour of Michael Chong's motion calling on the Standing Committee on Procedure and House Affairs to consider proposals to change Question Period.

In 1992, Peter Dobell and John Reid argued that Question Period reform was unlikely to happen.[81] The last twenty-five years validate their prediction, save for shorter questions and answers following the 1997 election. For all the energy that has been devoted to proposals and studies about reforming Question Period, there has been no progress toward achieving reform. The Standing Committee on House Management's report effectively collected dust after the 1993 election. The 2011 election ended the Standing Committee on Procedure and

---

78. Dobell and Reid, "A Larger Role for the House of Commons," 9.
79. Ibid.
80. Ryan, "Can Question Period Be Reformed?," 21.
81. Dobell and Reid, "A Larger Role for the House of Commons," 6.

House Affairs' study of Chong's proposed changes. Even the Liberal Party's modest campaign proposal in 2015 of introducing a Prime Minister's Question Period ceased to be a priority once the Liberals took office.

It raises the question of what can be done to achieve changes to the practices and procedures of Question Period. One reason, perhaps, that the 1993 report of the Standing Committee on House Management and Chong's 2010 motion have not resulted in changes to Question Period is that both recommended a package of sweeping reforms. While it was easy for MPs to vote in favour of Chong's motion for a Commons committee to study a package of changes, the lack of follow-through demonstrates that fundamentally changing the way Question Period operates is not a priority for most MPs. Although I believe there is widespread recognition that Question Period is not working the way that it should, there is a degree of comfort with the status quo. Also, Question Period is generally seen by opposition members as one of the few tools they have at their disposal to challenge the government, particularly in majority-government Parliaments. As Dobell and Reid accurately observed, "Unless and until there are significant changes in the way the House of Commons functions, which would restore some balance to the system, to ask the opposition leaders to give up some of the control they currently exercise over QP would be unfair. It would also be rejected."[82]

I believe that reforming Question Period will best be realized not through a package of reforms brought about all at once but through incremental change. In this regard, change may be achieved by individual members proposing specific changes. For example, the ban on clapping in the National Assembly of Quebec came about due to the efforts of the dean of the National Assembly, MNA François Gendron.[83] Reforming Question Period through the incremental efforts of individual members may not succeed; however, this would seem to be the best bet at this time in terms of realizing change.

---

82. Ibid, 6.
83. Perreaux, "Striking Silence Descends."

3

Empowering the Backbench:
The Story of Electronic Petitions

Kennedy Stewart

Something strange happened in the House of Commons on Wednesday, January 29, 2014. That evening, the Speaker called for a vote to be held on M-428, my private member's motion to bring electronic petitioning to Canada. As expected, Conservative prime minister Stephen Harper and his cabinet toed the party line and voted "nay," while all opposition members voted "yea." The motion should have gone down to defeat just like every other opposition party bill or motion put forward in the 41st Parliament because, after all, Harper controlled the majority of votes in the House. But that is not what happened. Harper failed to defeat my motion because eight of his Conservative backbenchers voted with me. It was the only vote he lost during his four-year majority government. As veteran parliamentary reporter Kady O'Malley wrote:

> In these days of majority Parliament, it's rare to find oneself impatiently waiting for the Speaker to read out the results of a vote. But that's exactly what happened on Wednesday night, when the fate of New Democrat MP Kennedy Stewart's bid to bring electronic petitions to the House of Commons was ultimately decided by the eight Conservative backbenchers who broke ranks with their caucus colleagues.

After a roll call vote that was too close to call based on eyeballs alone, it took several minutes for the clerks to tally the numbers. The reveal was delayed still further when Conservative MPs Diane Ablonczy and Michelle Rempel rose on points of order to make sure that their names were duly recorded amongst the nays.

There's no way to know if that was, in fact, the case, but as it turned out, it wouldn't have made a difference. In the end, the yeas had it, albeit by the narrowest of margins: 142 to 140.

The applause that followed the reading of the results drowned out the rest of the Speaker's words, and carried on for a full thirty seconds before the Speaker kindly but firmly called his charges back to order.

...for a motion officially opposed by the majority government to make it even this far is a victory for Stewart—and, indeed, for anyone who dreams of an alternate universe democratic chamber where votes don't so often go down along unwavering party lines.[84]

I tried to stay focused as the vote on almost three years of work unfolded that evening but soon lost count of the yes and no votes. I looked into the gallery, where my wife, Jeanette Ashe, was sitting and felt my stomach sink into my shoes as I thought I'd lost the vote. Some MPs who had said they would support me did not stand with the yeas, and it threw my concentration off. But then the Speaker announced that I had won. I won! I couldn't believe it. My colleagues cheered and slapped me on the back. We had finally found a way to beat Harper, uncovering a small weakness in his seemingly impregnable armour.

Even with the win I still had work to do, but after committee work the following year, another vote in the House approving the committee report (this time with unanimous support) determined that Canadians would have access to electronic petitioning starting with the 42nd Parliament. The very first national electronic petition was posted on December 4, 2015, calling for the government to ban the sale of electric

---

84. Kady O'Malley, "NDP Scores Surprise Win on E-petitions Thanks to 8 Tory MPs," CBC News, January 30, 2014, http://www.cbc.ca/news/politics/ndp-scores-surprise-win-on-e-petitions-thanks-to-8-tory-mps-1.2517292.

shock devices for pets. After gaining 5,421 signatures, the government issued an official response on May 30, 2016. As of December 12, 2016, over 500,000 Canadians had signed e-petitions on topics ranging from abandoned vessels to young people's health, as well as issues that have caused parties some discomfort by straying far from the House of Commons' tightly controlled agenda.

The story of e-petitioning demonstrates how minor changes to our political system can empower ordinary people and reinvigorate our politics. The tale of how e-petitioning came to be also shows how much work it takes to effect even a minor change to our system. The struggle for e-petitions illustrates how backbench members of Parliament can overcome the smothering reach and authority of political parties, and highlights why backbenchers need to fight for more freedom to represent their constituents.

The Crushing Power of Canadian Political Parties

One of the main themes of this book is the role political parties play in our democracy. As a starting point, Canadian political parties have more control over our politics than parties in any other democratic country. Many observers of Canadian politics agree, including Dr. Leslie Seidle of the Institute for Research on Public Policy, who states, "In the advanced parliamentary democracies, there is nowhere that has heavier, tighter party discipline than the Canadian House of Commons."[85] Indeed, individual Canadian members of Parliament are almost completely constrained from taking action outside what is determined by the leadership team of their political party.[86]

It is worth unpacking the idea of control to show what MPs are up against. There are two important aspects of control to consider: who controls the House of Commons' *agenda* and who controls how MPs *vote*. Agenda control is most important, as it allows parties to determine which issues are and are not discussed in the House. Government

---

85. Gloria Galloway, "Is Canada's Party Discipline the Strictest in the World? Experts Say Yes," *Globe and Mail*, February 7, 2013, http://www.theglobeandmail.com/news/politics/is-canadas-party-discipline-the-strictest-in-the-world-experts-say-yes/rticle8313261/.

86. *By leadership team I mean the party leader and other key MPs such as the whip and the House leader, as well as non-elected personnel such as leader's office and House leader's office staff. For the government, this would include the prime minister, House leader, whip and Prime Minister's Office.

and opposition parties wrestle to dominate what is discussed on any given day in the House of Commons, but at the same time MPs struggle within their own parties to determine what issues the party leadership will champion or bury in deep, dark holes. Parties also desperately try to control how MPs vote—to ensure all MPs vote with the party leader on all issues.

Party leadership teams use "party discipline" to exert control when setting agendas or votes. Disagree with the leadership team before an election and you will not be recruited or selected as a candidate. Take a contrary position during an election and you risk being dropped as a candidate. Speak out or vote against your party in the House of Commons and you'll be demoted in, or expelled from, the cabinet or shadow cabinet. Or maybe the party leadership team will ban you from asking questions in the House for six months or remove you from your favourite committee. Go too far and you'll get kicked out of the party caucus. MPs who find themselves even slightly offside with the party leadership team have very little opportunity to contribute to shaping the country, as almost all aspects of what happens in the Chamber are controlled by a small group surrounding the party leader, including the leader's principal secretary, the House leader, the whip, the national caucus chair and the leader's office's senior staff.

This was not always the case. Our politics were much different in the past. In fact, I doubt whether people today would recognize the House of Commons in the years following Confederation. For the first half-century of our parliamentary history, MPs would often vote with the party leader who promised them the most for their riding, regardless of which party they ran with during elections. Party lines were loose. According to Frank Underhill, "both front-benchers and backbenchers passed with remarkable ease from one political camp to another."[87] In terms of setting the agenda, House business was more or less evenly split between private members and government, giving ordinary MPs more control of which issues were debated and voted upon on the floor of the House of Commons.[88] In addition, while party

---

87. Frank H. Underhill, "The Development of National Political Parties in Canada," *Canadian Historical Review* 16, no. 4 (December 1935), 369.

88. Jean-François Godbout and Bjørn Høyland, "The Emergence of Parties in the Canadian House of Commons (1867–1908)," *Canadian Journal of Political Science* 46, no. 4 (December 2013).

leaders did what they could to convince—some would say bribe—MPs to vote with their party, this was far from guaranteed. As a result, government bills would often fail to pass, and party leaders would have to listen to the opinions of a wide array of MPs when changing laws or spending public money.

The power of individual MPs started to diminish during the early twentieth century as party leadership teams began to impose their wills in Parliament. Godbout and Høyland's exhaustive study of early voting in the House of Commons shows successive Liberal and Conservative governments decreased the amount of House time dedicated to private members' business and increased the time spent on government business. The less time spent on private members' business, the fewer opportunities for ordinary MPs to forward the concerns of their constituents.

Ordinary MPs started to resent their ebbing power to set the agenda, but their options to fight back were limited. As there were only two parties in the House of Commons—Liberals and Conservatives—even crossing the floor would not provide MPs with more time to talk about issues in their ridings, as the leadership teams of both parties worked to control the parliamentary agenda. As a result, frustrated MPs began to leave the two old parties to start new political parties such as the Progressive Party of Canada, formed in 1920, and the Co-operative Commonwealth Federation (CCF), formed in 1932. Ironically, as the number of parties represented in the House of Commons increased, so too did party discipline within *all* parties. As a result, while political candidates now have a larger array of political parties to join, they must now be ultra-loyal to whichever party team they end up standing with in order to keep their job.

The activities taking place during a typical day in the House of Commons illuminate this shift in priorities and opportunities. On most days, work officially starts with ministers tabling government bills or making statements. This is followed by a period in which ordinary MPs present private member's bills or motions and petitions (including, now, e-petitions). After government bill debate, the agenda shifts to MP statements and Question Period before moving back to discussing government bills. The day finishes with private members' business debates and starts all over again the next day, more or less following the same routine. [89]

Table 1: Agenda Setting and Leadership Team Control in Canada's House of Commons

Full Control	Partial Control	Little Control	Minutes	% of Day
Government Business			370	72%
Question Period			45	9%
	SO31 Members' Statements		15	3%
	Private Members' Business Debates		60	12%
		Private Members' Business Tabling	5	1%
		Petitions and E-petitions	15	3%
Total			510	100%
Full Leadership Team Control			415	81%
Partial Leadership Team Control			75	15%
Little Leadership Team Control			20	4%

Table 1 illustrates important categories of House of Commons business and estimates the amount of time allocated to the different opportunities ordinary MPs have to set the parliamentary agenda. Activities in which party leadership teams have *full control, partial control* or *little control* of the agenda are worth examining in more detail to get a sense of the party leadership teams' breadth of reach. Importantly, the table shows that individual MPs control only about 4 percent of the parliamentary agenda.

---

89. Robert Marleau and Camille Montpetit, eds., "The Daily Program," *House of Commons Procedure and Practice*, 2000, http://www.parl.gc.ca/marleaumont-petit/DocumentViewer.aspx?Sec=Ch10&Seq=3&Language=E.

Activities Where Party Leadership Teams Exert Full Agenda Control

On a typical day, MPs spend eight-and-a-half hours (510 minutes) debating the nation's business. Of this, over six hours (72%) of the agenda is directly controlled by the government leadership team, which oversees all aspects of government business including speech content. This holds for the opposition side of the House as well, where leadership teams decide who speaks and, for the most part, what is said in response to government initiatives.

Although the event attracts the most attention from the media and public hoping to see brilliance or MPs falling flat on their face, party leadership teams absolutely dominate what is said in the House of Commons during Question Period. The agenda of the forty-five minutes allotted to Question Period—9 percent of a typical day in the House— is mainly controlled by opposition party leadership teams that decide what questions will be asked, but also by the government leadership team, which decides what answers are given. Question Period really only reveals which ordinary MPs are better or worse at parroting the party line.

Activities Where Party Leadership Teams Exert Partial Agenda Control

The fifteen minutes before Question Period is reserved for MPs outside cabinet to make one-minute statements often called "Standing Order 31 statements," or SO31s. The content of these statements is mostly left to the members. However, the party leadership teams have final say on who speaks during these fifteen minutes and in some cases will not allow MPs to speak unless they comply with the will of the party.

A recent example of MP-muzzling comes from the Conservative Party. Backbench Conservative MPs informed the party leadership team of their intentions to make statements condemning the practice of sex-selective abortion, which is linked to their larger efforts to limit abortion in Canada. A number of backbench Conservative MPs— including BC's Mark Warawa and Saskatchewan's Leon Benoit—were scheduled to make their assigned one-minute statements but were then removed from the Speaker's list by the Conservative party leadership. I was in the House on the days when this kerfuffle was brewing and noticed the tension on the government benches. Benoit's account of party discipline outlines the power of the party leadership, even regarding House time specifically reserved for MPs to speak their mind: "I have had SO31s removed and I have been told that if I have one on a certain topic I simply will not be given SO31s."[90]

Leadership teams also retain partial control over the agenda when private members' business is debated. These five-per-week, one-hour segments of time are used to debate bills or motions put forward by MPs who are not in cabinet, on which the House of Commons will eventually vote. While most parties claim votes on these bills are not whipped—whereby MPs are forced to vote as the party leadership team dictates and the party whip enforces—the party leadership team decides who participates in these debates, and it provides speaking notes to which speakers are expected to adhere.

Activities Where Party Leadership Teams Exert Little Agenda Control

When the above activities are accounted for, party leadership teams have full or partial control over 96 percent of House of Commons proceedings. However there are two activities where party leadership teams struggle to control MPs: the five or so minutes allocated each day for MPs to introduce private members' business—either bills or motions—and the fifteen minutes when MPs present petitions. While often receiving little media coverage, these two activities can provide a glimpse of issues that MPs struggle to convince their parties to champion or not muzzle.

The most widely publicized and well-known tool for backbench MPs is the private member's bill. These are bills initiated by ordinary MPs that are drafted into statute form by the parliamentary legal team, giving them the apparent heft of any government bill. When presented to the House for first reading, MPs are provided time to make a short speech to introduce the bill. The vast majority of private member's bills never make it past first reading and are never voted upon. However, they are still useful, as MPs promote their bills and mini speeches through

---

90. Canadian Press and *National Post* Staff, "Conservative MP Says Mark Warawa and 'Rogue' Backbenchers Must 'Suffer the Consequences' for Anti-Abortion Stance," *National Post*, March 27, 2013, http://news.nationalpost.com/news/canada/canadian-politics/conservative-mp-says-mark-warawa-and-rogue-backbenchers-must-suffer-the-consequences-for-anti-abortion-stance.

regular and social media. There is no limit as to how many bills or motions individual members can forward, with many MPs taking full advantage of this freedom. Before retiring in 2015, NDP MP Libby Davies had thirty-three private member's bills on the order paper—ranging from implementing a national sodium restriction strategy to a Housing Bill of Rights. As will be explained later, the House does sometimes fully debate and vote on private member's bills.

Private member's motions are also important, as they allow a member to address an issue of concern without going through all the work of drafting a bill. For example, when affordable housing began to become a problem in British Columbia, I drafted an affordable housing strategy for the province in the form of a motion. This motion allowed me to promote an idea as to what could be done to address our housing problem, which I could present to the media and promote elsewhere. The drawbacks of private member's motions are that, unlike private member's bills, no time is allocated for members to speak to motions. Much like private member's bills, most motions never make it past the introductory stage. Just like private member's bills, the small number of private member's motions on which votes are cast can be impactful—I know, because my successful effort to introduce electronic petitions began as one!

Before initiating private member's bills or motions, most MPs will check with their party and their appropriate minister or critic to get a read on how the leadership team views the effort. In my experience, this is where many good ideas go to die. The member is told that the party does not approve of the initiative, and pressure is put on the member to drop the idea or promote something else. This is often enough to kill the effort, but sometimes members persist and air their ideas in public.

MPs are allocated a minute or so to speak when they present petitions to the House of Commons. Before the introduction of e-petitions, these requests for action could only be written on paper and submitted to the House if they had twenty-five or more original signatures from Canadian citizens or residents of Canada. Both paper and e-petitions allow ordinary MPs to momentarily take control of the agenda, as the party leadership team does not dictate the topic of the petition or what the member says when the petition is presented to the House. While many petitions originate from members of the public, MPs often create their own petitions in order to raise an issue in the House.

An example of working outside the official frame comes from my work to stop a crude oil pipeline from being built through my constituency. In this case, I worked with local residents to craft a petition calling on the prime minister to block Texas oil giant Kinder Morgan's new project and presented this petition many times in the House, even when my own party's leadership team would have preferred that I did not raise the issue. Conservative Party members often create and present anti-abortion petitions against the wishes of their party leadership. As with private member's bills and motions, we make our speeches, record the CPAC television broadcast and use social media to promote our cause.

The E-Petitioning Story

With leadership teams exerting so much control over the parliamentary agenda, it is no surprise many backbench MPs take advantage of the opportunity to table petitions and private member's bills and motions. Most backbenchers even experience a "golden moment" when the Speaker calls one of their bills or motions for debate and a vote. While the prime minister's leadership team decides when government bills are called for debate, private members' business is debated according to an order of precedence established by a random draw of MP names. One of the most exciting moments for all backbench MPs occurs at the beginning of each parliamentary session when the clerk of the House conducts this lottery.

After my May 2, 2011, election, my name was drawn ninetieth out of a list of 240 in the June lottery. This meant that I would have the opportunity to force MPs to vote yea or nay on virtually any idea I chose. Many MPs drawing later numbers didn't get a chance to have their ideas voted upon, as we simply ran out of time during the four-year period between elections. When my number was drawn I took it very seriously; I knew I had the privilege of having the highest law-making body in the land consider my proposal.

I first decided that my private member's bill or motion had to be something near and dear to my heart, since it would take a lot of effort to get something passed and I had to really believe in what I was doing. Having written my master's and PhD theses on democratic reform besides having dedicated almost twenty years of my life to the topic as a political science professor, I decided that the vote I would attempt to trigger would have to involve improving Canadian democracy.

I also decided that my bill would have to have a chance of winning a majority of votes in the House, and that meant securing votes from all NDP, Liberal, Green and Bloc members as well as at least a few Conservatives. In 2011, the Conservatives had 166 of 308 seats (54%), the NDP had 103 (33%), the Liberals 34 (11%), the Bloc 4 (1%) and the Green Party 1 (0.3%). In order to win a vote, I would have to secure 50 percent plus one of the votes from the MPs sitting in the House at the time my vote was called. So if all MPs were present and I was able to secure the support from all of the opposition parties, my vote would still fail 166 to 142 if all government MPs showed up and voted nay. Despite the promise of "free votes" on private members' business by party leaders, almost every single private member's bill vote falls according to party lines.

I had just been an MP for a month when this opportunity presented itself, with a new job to learn, lots of new colleagues to meet, two offices to set up and talented but new staff to train. So what to propose? What bill could I draft that would advance Canadian democracy that would have a chance to pass? Triggering a referendum on proportional representation? Nope, there was no way the Conservatives or Liberals would go for that. Setting aside Senate seats for indigenous peoples? The Liberals might go for it, but Harper and his majority of votes would not. I found myself stuck for ideas in those early days of the session.

Luckily my wife, Dr. Jeanette Ashe, is also a political scientist who's dedicated to improving our democracy. Jeanette spends much of her time researching and writing about British politics, and she was the first to bring up the electronic petitioning system used in the UK. Brought in by Labour prime minister Tony Blair in 2006 and continued by all subsequent prime ministers, the UK e-petitioning system was largely seen as a success and a step forward for democracy, as it gives ordinary people more control over the parliamentary agenda. The first iteration of British e-petitioning allowed citizens to create and sign petitions online, with the government issuing official responses to all petitions receiving at least five hundred signatures.[91] The system became so popular it was modified in 2011 by Conservative prime minister David Cameron so that only petitions gaining ten thousand signatures would

91. Scott A. Hale, Helen Margetts, and Taha Yasseri, "Petition Growth and Success Rates on the UK No. 10 Downing Street Website," Proceedings of the 5th Annual ACM Web Science Conference (WebSci 2013).

receive a response from the government, but also that any petition gaining 100,000 or more signatures would be considered for a debate in Parliament.

I then had to decide what form my proposal would take: a private member's bill or a private member's motion. My legislative assistant Michelle Silongan began a conversation with the House of Commons clerk in charge of paper petitions, Olivier Champagne. He informed us that the proper procedure would be to put forward a private member's motion as opposed to a bill, since I was not trying to change a law, but rather the procedures by which the House of Commons performs its duties—known as standing orders. Champagne also informed us that other MPs had tried, and failed, to bring electronic petitions to the House of Commons since 2003. I knew I had my work cut out for me.

In February 2012, I crafted and tabled a very detailed motion outlining how the Procedure and House Affairs committee (PROC) should alter the standing orders to allow Canadians to create and sign petitions online, with petitions having fifty thousand or more signatures automatically triggering a debate in the House of Commons. Motion 318 was drafted with help from my wife, Jeanette, Simon Fraser University professors Paddy Smith and Andrew Heard, Dr. Ruth Fox of the United Kingdom's Hansard Society, NDP staff researchers, my office staff and the House of Commons legal team. Once the motion was tabled, twenty NDP MPs jointly seconded it—a good omen that e-petitions would at least have the support of my colleagues.

However later that year Stéphanie Haché, a highly competent NDP staff person in charge of overseeing private members' business, convinced me that Motion 318 needed considerable redrafting or it would fail to secure support with MPs from other parties. She suggested that the wording be changed from instructing the Procedure and House Affairs committee in exactly how to implement e-petitions to calling on the committee to conduct a study of them. This might seem like a massive weakening of the effort, but the new motion, 428, was written to include a deadline for the study's completion, and most importantly it maintained the direction of "how" to establish e-petitions, not "if." Thus, while the motion appeared to be a mere study, it actually guaranteed implementation of some form of electronic petitions if it was passed. Tabled on February 13, 2013, Motion 428 was as follows:

That the Standing Committee on Procedure and House Affairs be instructed to recommend changes to the Standing Orders and other conventions governing petitions so as to establish an electronic petitioning system that would enhance the current paper-based petitions system by allowing Canadians to sign petitions electronically, and to consider, among other things, (i) the possibility to trigger a debate in the House of Commons outside of current sitting hours when a certain threshold of signatures is reached, (ii) the necessity for no fewer than five Members of Parliament to sponsor the e-petition and to table it in the House once a time limit to collect signatures is reached, (iii) the study made in the 38th Parliament regarding e-petitions, and that the Committee report its findings to the House, with proposed changes to the Standing Orders and other conventions governing petitions, within twelve months of the adoption of this order.

Knowing I had most of my NDP colleagues onside, I started thinking about how to win votes from MPs in other parties. My mind kept going back to my doctoral supervisor Professor Keith Dowding's tutelage. A noted rational choice expert, Keith had drilled into my head that I had to figure out people's preferences and then appeal to their self-interest. Using this logic, I thought at least Green Party Leader Elizabeth May and most Liberal MPs would support the motion, as they often spoke about improving democracy, but the Conservatives would be a challenge. Securing votes from all opposition MPs would give me only 44 percent of the votes in the House. I required at least another 6 percent to win. This would be tough, as Harper ruled his party with an iron fist and was not about to let the NDP control any part of the agenda, let alone push forward a reform.

I needed to find a crack in Harper's formidable fortifications, so I turned to his backbench. Research showed that a number of backbench Conservative MPs had put forward their own democratic reform proposals. In addition, many were past members of Preston Manning's Reform Party—a party that had supported populist measures such as referendums, initiatives and recalls. I saw these actions and affiliations as strong clues as to which Conservative MPs might be persuaded to split from their leader and vote for my motion. I had to convince them that supporting my democratic reform motion was more important than earning brownie points from Harper.

My first call was to Conservative Saskatchewan MP Brad Trost, whom I had gotten to know through committee work. Trost is a well-known social conservative whose views on abortion and other issues are the polar opposite to my own. He seemed independently minded and, more importantly, he had his own democratic reform private member's motion to better empower backbench MPs on standing committees. On Valentine's Day 2013, Brad publicly supported me by jointly seconding M-428, signing his name along with eighteen of my NDP colleagues. To show my gratitude, I jointly seconded his motion for committee reform. I remember the day this happened— our deputy whip literally followed me around the House of Commons to make sure I didn't sign it. I did anyway. Buoyed by Trost's support, I approached backbench Conservative MP Brent Rathgeber, who also jointly seconded my motion.

With my own caucus and two backbench Conservatives aboard, I began to think how I could gain even more support from Harper's team. I decided to move outside Parliament and try to secure the endorsements of famous democratic reformers. My first port of call was former NDP leader Ed Broadbent, who gave me a supportive celebrity quote, for which I am grateful. I knew Broadbent's support would not hold much water with Conservatives, so I decided to approach the Reform Party icon Preston Manning. To my surprise, Manning moved past partisanship and endorsed my idea of bringing electronic petitioning to Canada. By grouping these two endorsements, I managed to get a great story in the *Vancouver Sun* and most Postmedia papers on February 26, 2013. E-petitioning had legs!

Importantly, *Vancouver Sun* reporter Peter O'Neil and his editors decided this odd-couple story of Stewart and Trost, Broadbent and Manning would interest their readers and was worth following over the longer term. I had my hook, but had to keep it going. In the coming months I secured support from the Canadian Centre for Policy Alternatives as well as their ideological counterpart, the Canadian Taxpayers Federation. Supporters also included the Canadian Federation of Students, Samara Canada, OpenMedia, Egale, LeadNow and the Canadian Association of Retired People. It wasn't all sunshine, though. Requests to support my motion were rejected by the Fraser

Institute, Naomi Klein, John Manley, Kim Campbell, Stephen Lewis, Mothers Against Drunk Driving and others.

In order to gain even more press coverage, I commissioned Angus Reid Public Opinion to conduct Canada-wide polling on the topic at the end of March 2013. Survey results showed 81 percent of those surveyed responded positively when asked, "Do you support or oppose allowing Canadians to use electronic petitions to present their requests to the federal government?" More news stories followed. With polling, MP endorsements, NGO support and media coverage, I felt I was ready to make a strong and positive case for e-petitions as we moved to the first hour of debate in the House of Commons.

The first hour of debate, on June 12, 2013, was revealing, as it showed where I had secured support and where I had more work to do. After my introductory speech, Conservative MP Dave MacKenzie rose to give the government's response to my idea, which concluded, "I am going to oppose Motion No. 428, and I call on all members to do likewise."[92] Conservative MP Scott Armstrong gave a speech in which he concluded that he was not prepared to vote for my motion. While my heart sank upon hearing these words, it was soon buoyed by those of Liberal critic of democratic reform Stéphane Dion, who stated, "The Liberal caucus supports the motion and commends the member who brought it forward. We support it because we agree with the principle of electronic petitions and because the hon. member for Burnaby–Douglas had the wisdom not to ask the House to adopt this measure before it was carefully examined in committee out of respect for the role of the committee and the House."

Between June 2013 and January 2014 I worked to convince Conservative backbenchers to support my motion with help from my new staff member Andrew Cuddy, who made it his mission to get M-428 passed. I had spoken with Green Party leader Elizabeth May and knew I would receive her and Bruce Hyer's support (Hyer had left the NDP to join the Green Party caucus). I had struck up a growing friendship with Conservative MP Michael Chong, who was championing his own private member's bill, popularly known as the *Reform Act*, which sought to reduce the power of party leaders. As Chong's goals were

---

92. Canada, *House of Commons Debates*, 41st Parliament, 1st Session, Hansard no. 268, June 12, 2013, http://www.parl.gc.ca/HousePublications/ Publication.aspx?Language=E&Mode=1&Parl=41&Ses=1&DocId=6208895.

broadly in line with my own, I jointly seconded his bill and worked to secure support for his effort within the NDP caucus with the hope that he would return the favour within his own caucus.

While my second hour of debate was scheduled for October 2013, Prime Minister Harper's September 13, 2013, decision to prorogue Parliament shifted the parliamentary schedule. As a result, my motion was not debated for a second time until January 27, 2014.[93] The second hour of debate went much like the first had. NDP MPs Charmaine Borg, Laurin Liu, Robert Aubin and Murray Rankin made spirited appeals to the Conservatives to support e-petitions, as did Liberal Kevin Lamoureux, while Conservative MP Joe Preston repeated his party's opposition.

The January 29, 2014, vote was a very dramatic and unexpected 142–140 win. Twenty-five MPs were absent, leaving 283 votes to be counted. The NDP, Liberals, Bloc and Greens all voted "yea," while the Conservatives all voted against, with the exception of Leon Benoit, Garry Breitkreuz, Michael Chong, James Rajotte, Kyle Seeback, Brad Trost, Maurice Vellacott, John Williamson and Rob Anders (who abstained). I had expected support from Benoit, Breitkreuz, Chong, Rajotte, Trost and Vellacott, as well as Conservative MPs Larry Miller and Bruce Stanton. Miller and Stanton sadly backed out and voted with Harper. I had not expected support from Seeback and Williamson but later discovered they had close links with Gregory Thomas of the Canadian Taxpayers Federation, who had publicly endorsed my motion. Why Anders abstained I do not know, but because he turned his back on the prime minister during the vote I assume it was some personal beef that kept him seated. I will always be grateful to NDP MP Robert Chisholm, who cancelled a medical procedure to attend the vote, and NDP MP François Lapointe for driving fourteen hours to make sure his name was counted.

Watching MPs vote yea or nay, the evening quickly became a blur. Speaker Andrew Scheer also lost track of things at one point, when he asked the clerk for instructions as to what to do in the event of a tie. MPs stood and sat down. Cabinet members demanded their votes be properly recorded. I received nervous glances from my colleagues, and angry

---

93. Canada, *House of Commons Debates*, 41st Parliament, 2nd Session, Hansard no. 35, January 27, 2014, http://www.parl.gc.ca/HousePublications/Publication.aspx?Language=e&Mode=1&Parl=41&Ses=2&DocId=6391978.

looks and words were exchanged between Conservatives. And then the win! E-petitions passed. Beyond the win itself, another highlight for me was when Prime Minister Harper turned to his House leader, Peter Van Loan, and spat out, "What the fuck happened?"

With success in the House, the motion proceeded to the Standing Committee on Procedure and House Affairs (PROC), which was chaired by Conservative MP Joe Preston. While Preston had spoken and voted against my motion, he was known as a fair player and maintained that reputation throughout the committee review of it. My main opponent on the committee was Conservative Tom Lukiwski, whom I knew would be tough but also had a reputation for being reasonable. Lucky for me I had NDP stalwarts David Christopherson, Craig Scott and Alexandrine Latendresse to help steer things through. Over the course of eight meetings, the committee heard from thirteen witnesses representing House of Commons staff, the Canadian Taxpayers Federation, the National Assembly of Quebec, the Legislative Assembly of the Northwest Territories, Samara Canada, the UK's Hansard Society, Dr. Catherine Bochel from the University of Lincoln in the UK, the Office of the Leader of the House of Commons of the UK, the UK's Cabinet Office and the UK's House of Commons Procedure Committee.

While some of the discussion centred on technical details such as security and data retention, the core consideration was whether to implement a system by which petitions with a large number of signatures—maybe 50,000 or 100,000—would automatically trigger a debate in the House of Commons. The Conservatives made it clear they would find a way to undo the whole effort unless I dropped this condition. However, they also agreed to support a more minimalist e-petitioning system if this clause were removed.

When I was first drafting M-428 I had a suspicion that if I somehow got to committee I would need to make concessions to the Conservatives. So I purposely built the motion like a rocket—with stages that I could jettison in order to save the nose cone. During the committee hearings I agreed to drop the idea of e-petitions triggering debates provided that a clause would be added stipulating that the rules would be reviewed two years after the system was implemented. The Conservatives agreed and also included a condition that at least one member of Parliament would be required to officially sponsor an e-petition for it to be posted on the government website, so as to cut down on frivolous use of the system. The report was sent back to the House and on March 11, 2015, it was unanimously adopted. Four years of hard work had paid off, and e-petitioning was born against all odds.

The Impact of E-petitions

After the House of Commons agreed to implement electronic petitions, House of Commons staff put in place the infrastructure needed to have the system up and running after the October 2015 election. E-1 (Cruelty to Animals) was posted on December 4, 2015, by Gwendy Williams, a constituent of mine who wanted a ban on the use of shock collars on pets. I agreed to sponsor the petition, and Gwendy and her husband, Alfie, worked hard to promote the idea—including garnering financial support from cosmetics giant Lush. They managed to secure 5,421 signatures, well past the 500-signature threshold needed to trigger an official response from Justin Trudeau's new Liberal government. On April 11, 2016, justice minister Jody Wilson-Raybould replied, "the government agrees that animal cruelty laws should send a strong and clear message that animal cruelty is totally unacceptable in our society." This response was emailed to those who had signed the petition, and the Williamses and their cause appeared in many national and local news stories. While the government did not enact the requested change, the petition had encouraged thousands of Canadians to take political action, and the media attention increased awareness of the cause.

Table 2: E-petitions in Canada: Quality Over Quantity, December 14, 2015–December 12, 2016

Category	Number	% of Submitted	% of Approved	% of Closed (120 days)
Submitted	712	100%		
Approved	209	29%	100%	
Still open for signatures	59		28%	
Closed after 120 days	150		72%	100%
Passed 500-signature threshold	116		56%	77%

Table 2 traces the first year of e-petitioning and reveals three important things. First, Canadians have begun to access this new democratic tool in droves, with 712 e-petitions initiated by the public—almost two per day since the service began. Second, the safeguards in the system are working to ensure Canadians are asked to sign only well thought-out ideas. Only 209 (29%) of submitted e-petitions met the technical requirements and received sponsorship from a member of Parliament. Third, Canadians are keen to support these high-quality e-petitions. Of those approved e-petitions that have been closed after reaching the 120-day time limit to acquire signatures, a whopping 116 (77%) received the five hundred or more signatures required to qualify for a government response. So far the system is delivering quality, not quantity.

Table 3: E-petitions and Political Parties, December 14, 2015–December 12, 2016

Party	Petitions	Seats	Average per MP
Green	12	1	12.00
NDP	67	44	1.52
Bloc Québécois	6	10	0.60
Conservatives	52	97	0.54
Liberals	72	180	0.40
Independents	0	1	0.00
Vacant	0	5	0.00
Total	209	338	0.62

Table 3 shows opposition MPs submit more e-petitions than those sitting on the government side of the House. When looking at the 209 approved e-petitions on a per party basis, Elizabeth May's member-of-one Green Party has generated the most petitions per MP, followed by the NDP with almost one-and-a-half petitions per MP in the first year of the program. The Conservatives and the Bloc have yet to fully embrace this system, although it is important to keep in mind the Bloc usually confines itself to activities in Quebec.

If the UK experience is any guide, we can expect many more Canadians to submit e-petitions in the future. The UK system started slowly and then took off once the system became better known. That the

Canadian system promotes quality over quantity is also a step forward for e-petitioning—with frivolous petitions being kept to a minimum. On a personal note, I couldn't be more pleased with how the system is progressing now that I see the effort has gone some ways to reducing Canada's democratic deficit.

What Needs to Change?

The e-petition story provides a model for how the House of Commons can function more democratically. With e-petitions, my team put forward a well-researched and considered private member's proposal and canvassed all MPs for support in good faith, regardless of their political stripe. In return, many non-NDP MPs took off their party hats and supported my motion. In lending full caucus support, the Liberals, Bloc and Greens took a small risk in supporting an idea from a member of a party with which they would compete for votes in future elections. This showed a willingness to throw off partisan cloaks to improve democracy.

Opposition MPs risked no repercussions from their party leadership teams, since e-petitioning was supported by party leaders. The real risk-takers were the backbench Conservatives who jeopardized their future advancement within the party when they voted for my motion. Private discussions revealed all of them suffered in one way or another for voting the way they did, as I did within my party for supporting and jointly seconding their bills and motions. I think most Canadians would agree this seems wrong and needs to change.

Zooming back out to the larger picture of how our parliamentary democracy works, if we transported an MP sitting in the House of Commons in 1867 through time to the present day, that MP would not recognize the procedures followed in today's House of Commons and would be shocked at how little freedom there is to raise local issues. Likewise, a twenty-first century MP transported back to the post-Confederation Commons would likely get lost in the leeway and independence. Put these time-travelling MPs together to discuss their experiences and I am sure they would agree that a better balance must be struck between a House of Commons where MPs are so independent that the country is ungovernable and a House where MPs cannot even sit or stand without permission from their party leaders.

One way to lessen party control would be to allocate more time for private members' business, which has shrunk to a mere 4 percent of time spent in the House of Commons. This time should be increased so at the very least every backbench MP has the opportunity to have an idea voted upon—or even better, every backbench MP has the opportunity to trigger votes on two bills or motions. Although this change would cut into the time for debating government bills, the result would better empower ordinary MPs.

While increasing the time spent on private members' business would give backbench MPs more airtime, it would do little to fix the smothering party discipline. Unleashing backbenchers requires weakening the grip of party leadership teams. Michael Chong's *Reform Act* was an important first step in further empowering ordinary MPs. For one, its clauses can give MPs, not the party leader, final say over who sits in the party caucus and stops party leaders from unilaterally kicking MPs out of the party. Second, it gives MPs the power to trigger a leadership review vote to remove an overly controlling party leader. Finally, it removes the ability of party leaders to block candidates from running for their party. While Chong beat the odds and succeeded in getting his private member's bill passed into law, the parties have not fully embraced these changes, and things remain much as they were. If this does not change in future Parliaments, revisiting the *Reform Act* would seem a very good idea.

Regarding e-petitions, the final section of the Procedure and House Affairs committee (PROC) report states that PROC should undertake a review of the system and process after it has operated for two years—sometime after December 2017. This review should be undertaken and it is my view that we should continue to broadly follow the UK e-petition model. As per my original motion, e-petitions should be debated in the House of Commons if they gain over a certain number of signatures. Only forty-seven petitions in the UK have surpassed the 100,000-signature threshold, with only thirty-one being debated. As our population is roughly half that of the UK, a 50,000–signature threshold would be more appropriate for triggering debates here in Canada. However, the signature threshold for triggering a government response should not be raised from five hundred to ten thousand as in the UK. Unlike the UK system, the Canadian one requires an MP to sponsor an e-petition before it is posted on the website. As such, a much smaller percentage of e-petitions are approved to go live in our country. The current signature threshold should be maintained so as to empower as many Canadians as possible to participate.

In conclusion, this chapter shows the power of ordinary MPs has greatly diminished over the years as party leadership teams have reduced the time allocated to private members' business in order to exert more central party control over the parliamentary agenda. The story of e-petitions illustrates how difficult it has become for backbenchers to control even a small fraction of the agenda and contribute to making Canada a more democratic and better place to live. It also shows that reaching across the "two sword lengths" separating the government and opposition benches can work if the effort is genuine, and that additional reforms should be enacted to unleash the promise of the backbench.

Rebalancing Power in Ottawa: Committee Reform

Michael Chong

A t the heart of Canada's democracy is the House of Commons, currently made up of 338 elected members of Parliament (MPs), as of 2016. This is where the people's representatives do their work, and it is the only place at the national level where Canadians are democratically represented. It is important to note why the role of MP is so important in the Canadian system. In many other democracies, such as the United States, citizens exercise three votes at the national level: a vote for president, a vote for the senate and a vote for the house. Citizens in the American republic have three democratic avenues to pursue when they want to voice their concerns, which is true of many other democracies as well.

However, citizens exercise only one vote at the national level in Canada: a vote for their local MP. Canadians rightfully expect their local member to be able to respond to their concerns. Unfortunately, the reality of Ottawa is that real power is held by only a few of the 338 elected MPs—in particular, party leaders and the prime minister. This was not always the case. At Confederation, elected MPs wielded a great deal more power than they do today. MPs were referred to as "loose fish," an allusion to the accepted fact that MPs were not under the control of party leaders or the prime minister.

Our present system of parliamentary democracy has changed a lot over the years. Rule changes within the House of Commons, changes in elections law and the increasing power of political parties have all contributed to the diminished role of the MP and the increased power of party leaders, particularly the prime minister. There has been much talk over the years about addressing this problem and reining in the power of party leaders while strengthening the role of elected MPs and the House of Commons as a whole.

One of the wonderful aspects of our system is it was not created in a vacuum. It rests on a foundation of nearly one thousand years of British parliamentary tradition, a tradition of good government that has been exported to many other parts of the world. As a result, we have many other Westminster-style parliaments to compare ourselves with. In this chapter we will compare and contrast the Canadian parliament's committee system with that of the "mother" British parliament in the Palace of Westminster in London.

Compared to the British parliament, it is clear that the Canadian system gives party leaders, particularly the prime minister, much more power over MPs. In the 1997 British parliament, a majority of backbench Labour MPs voted against the Labour government on 104 occasions. In the 2001 British parliament, a majority of backbench Labour MPs voted against the Labour government 21 percent of the time; in the 2005 British parliament, the figure was 28 percent. The trend has continued in the 2010 British parliament with a majority of backbench Conservative MPs voting against the Tory government more than one-third of the time. The autonomy exercised by MPs in the UK is unheard of in Canada. In the Canadian parliament, the average compliance of backbench government MPs with their whip is over 99 percent. The same is true of opposition parties. Clearly, greater freedom from party-leader power is needed for elected MPs in the Canadian House of Commons; this would allow MPs who are not in cabinet to fulfill their constitutional role in holding government to account.

One area that should be the focus of rebalancing power between party leaders and MPs is the committee system of the House of Commons. The committee system is at the heart of the day-to-day functioning of the Commons. This is where much of the work is done by MPs: legislation is amended, and government spending and taxation are approved. Currently committees are made up of small groups of MPs, usually ten, and are created by the Commons, usually through standing orders. There are a number of different types of committees. The majority are permanent, while some are established for a temporary period of time. Committees are made up of MPs from the formally "recognized parties" in the House of Commons (parties that have at least twelve MPs in the House). For most MPs, committee work occupies the vast majority of their time in Parliament. For example, in fiscal year 2007–08, committees held nearly 1,200 meetings, representing nearly 1,700 hours of work. In contrast, the Commons held 113 sittings during the same period.

As the modern state emerged and expanded, committees emerged because it was becoming too cumbersome and inefficient for the House to handle the increasing volume and complexity of legislation, government spending and other matters. It was far more effective to perform this work in smaller groups than in a legislative assembly of more than three hundred members. There are other benefits of the committee system. Members who remain on a particular committee for a period of time develop expertise in a particular policy field. Members also engage more meaningfully with the individuals and groups that are called to appear and testify in front of committee, thus drawing the House of Commons closer to the people it is supposed to represent.

A reform that would go a long way toward rebalancing power between party leaders and MPs would be to remove the power of party leaders, including the prime minister, to decide the membership of committees. Giving that power to MPs on a secret ballot vote at the beginning of a new Parliament would allow committees greater autonomy to amend legislation, review spending and hold the government to account. Another reform that would give committees greater autonomy would be to elect committee chairs by secret ballot vote. Finally, reducing the number of committees would make more effective use of MPs' time.

From a procedural point of view, these reforms would be easy to implement. It would simply require a motion to be passed in the Commons to amend the standing orders that concern the selection of committee membership, the election of committee chairs and the mandates of committees. (Standing orders are the permanent written rules by which the House of Commons regulates its proceedings. Since they do not lapse at the end of a session of Parliament, they are "standing." There are about 150 standing orders.) Whether the political will exists to make this reform a reality is another matter. However, there is some cause for optimism. In the last few years, the UK's House of Commons has introduced successful reforms to its committee system.

A Brief History

Canada's parliamentary system of government began long before July 1, 1867. The legislatures of Upper and Lower Canada, their successor legislature in the United Province of Canada, and the legislatures in Nova Scotia and New Brunswick all possessed sophisticated systems of parliamentary government well before Confederation. In fact, the first elected legislature in what is now Canada was established in Halifax on October 2, 1758, when the Nova Scotia House of Assembly, which consisted of twenty-two men, met for the first time. What these systems of parliamentary government all had in common was their origin in British parliamentary tradition.

Committees of the British parliament began in the fourteenth century with the responsibility of drawing up legislation in response to petitions. By the sixteenth century, committees had become a regular part of Parliament, tasked with amending legislation that the House of Commons had agreed to in principle. Committees also considered politically charged and contentious matters: there was the Committee for the Uniformity of Religion in 1571, and the Committee on the Queen of Scots in 1572—a committee concerned with Mary, Queen of Scots, in prison at the time and subsequently beheaded.

While some committees were effectively permanent, such as the threateningly named Grand Committee for Evils that existed in 1623, most committees were temporary in nature. This pattern of establishing an ad hoc committee for a particular matter continued well into the twentieth century. By the 1830s, the legislatures of Upper and Lower Canada began to establish permanent committees, or "standing committees," as opposed to the previous practice of establishing ad hoc committees as the need arose. When the new Dominion of Canada was established in 1867, there were ten standing committees with rules based on what was in place in the United Province of Canada:

- Privileges and Elections
- Expiring Laws

- Railways
- Canals and Telegraph Lines
- Miscellaneous Private Bills
- Standing Orders
- Printing
- Public Accounts
- Banking and Commerce
- Immigration and Colonization

The number of standing committees has grown substantially since then, while the number of members who sit on a committee has shrunk. At the time of Confederation, committee membership was drawn up by a committee "comprised of leading men of the ministry and opposition." All members were given a day or two to examine the lists compiled by this committee before being asked to approve the report. In the early years after Confederation, standing committees were quite large, with some having over a hundred members. Since quorum required a majority (or a substantial number) to be present to conduct business, this made it challenging for many committees to get work done. As a result, the number of members on a committee was reduced over the years. By the 1960s the largest standing committee had a membership of fifteen. By 2016 that number had declined to ten.

From Confederation to the 1960s, standing committees did not meet regularly. Most Commons business was conducted by the House sitting as a committee of the whole. By the late 1960s business that had once been conducted by committees of the whole, such as approval of government spending and amendments to government legislation, was delegated to the various standing committees. In the 1980s standing committees gained the power to initiate their own studies and inquiries concerning departments relevant to their mandates.

Committees in Today's House of Commons

Committees of the House of Commons may be permanent or ad hoc (established for a specific purpose and disbanded once it has been fulfilled). Standing committees, standing joint committees and the liaison committee are examples of the former; committees of the whole, legislative committees, special committees and special joint committees are examples of the latter. Setting aside committees of the whole (as they often exist for mere minutes), in 2016 there were thirty committees of the House of Commons: twenty-seven permanent and three ad hoc. The membership of most committees consists exclusively of members of the House of Commons. However, a few have mixed membership consisting of members from both the House and the Senate. These committees are called "joint" committees. Committees vary in the number of members, with most consisting of ten.

As mentioned, a committee of the whole is an ad hoc committee made up of the entire membership of the House of Commons. While the memberships of the House and a committee of the whole are identical, and while they both meet in the main chamber, the rules governing each are different. While the House of Commons is presided over by the Speaker, the committee of the whole is presided over by the deputy speaker, who assumes the role of the chair. A committee of the whole is created to deal with a specific matter, and once the matter at hand has been dealt with, the committee ceases to exist. Over the course of a year, many committees of the whole are created and disbanded. Little time is spent sitting as a committee of the whole, since the present practice is to use a committee of the whole to quickly pass legislation.

Legislative committees and special committees are two other types of ad hoc committees. Legislative committees are created to review and amend a particular bill. Special committees are created to carry out a specific inquiry or study, rather than review and amend legislation. For example, two special committees were established in 2016: one on pay equity and the other on electoral reform. Special joint committees are another type of ad hoc committee temporarily established for a particular purpose. In 2015 the special joint committee on physician-assisted dying was created to review and make recommendations for a federal response to the Supreme Court's *Carter v. Canada* decision.

Standing joint committees are permanent committees consisting of members of both the House of Commons and the Senate. In 2016, there were two standing joint committees: the Standing Joint Committee on the Library of Parliament and the Standing Joint Committee for the Scrutiny of Regulations. Of all the committees, the most important are the standing committees. These permanent committees are where the vast majority of committee work is done and where MPs spend a lot of time. Standing committees also make up the bulk of committees in the House of Commons, with twenty-four in existence in 2016. The last type of permanent committee is the liaison committee. While not a standing committee, it is made up of the chairs of all the standing committees and the Commons chairs of the standing joint committees. The liaison committee is responsible for allocating funds to the standing committees for their operations.

The Power of Committees

Committees have the ability to examine and investigate all matters within their mandate. They have the right to call witnesses—both individuals and groups—to testify and provide evidence. The vast majority of these witnesses are eager to appear to present their views on the public record; however, there are occasions when an invited witness is unwilling to appear in front of committee. In this case, the committee has the power to summon such a witness to appear, a right inherited from the UK House of Commons when the British North America Act (1867) came into effect. This power reflects Parliament's position as one of the highest courts of the land. In 2007, the Standing Committee on Access to Information, Privacy and Ethics requested that the Speaker issue any necessary warrants for the appearance of businessman Karlheinz Schreiber. As a result, Schreiber was transferred from provincial prison at the Toronto West Detention Centre to the Ottawa–Carleton Detention Centre and subsequently appeared before committee on November 29, 2007. Another constitutional privilege delegated to all committees is the power to request and obtain evidence from individuals and organizations. Evidence can consist of oral testimony, written materials, photographs, audio recordings or videos. In both the House and in committees, members and witnesses enjoy a broader right to freedom of speech than in the "real world," permitting them to speak without inhibition and have immunity from criminal prosecution or civil liability.

Standing Committees

Standing committees can be categorized into three areas of focus. There are committees that oversee a particular department or organization. These committees can be said to be "vertical" committees, as they hold the government accountable from the top to the bottom of a particular department or organization. Then there are committees that oversee matters relevant to the whole government. These committees can be said to be "horizontal," as they hold the government accountable for its activities across the whole of government. Finally, there are committees that are responsible for Commons administration and procedure. The standing committees as of September 2016 are as follows:

- Veterans Affairs
- Agriculture and Agri-Food
- Canadian Heritage
- International Trade
- Citizenship and Immigration
- Environment and Sustainable Development
- Access to Information, Privacy and Ethics
- Foreign Affairs and International Development
- Status of Women
- Finance
- Fisheries and Oceans
- Health
- Human Resources, Skills and Social Development and the Status of Persons with Disabilities
- Indigenous and Northern Affairs
- Industry, Science and Technology
- Justice and Human Rights
- Official Languages
- National Defence
- Government Operations and Estimates
- Public Accounts
- Procedure and House Affairs
- Natural Resources
- Public Safety and National Security
- Transport, Infrastructure and Communities

Usually, standing committees consist of ten members. The seats on a committee are allocated in proportion to the recognized party standings in the House of Commons. As of September 2016, the seat allocation was as follows:

Recognized Party	Seats in the House of Commons	Seats on a Standing Committee
Liberal	182	6
Conservative	97	3
NDP	44	1

Most MPs are members of at least one standing committee, and some are members of two. It is rare that an MP would be a regular member of three or more standing committees, because of the heavy workload that would entail. Normally the Speaker, deputy speaker, ministers (including the prime minister) and party leaders are not members of committees. Parliamentary secretaries are usually members of the standing committee that concerns their areas of responsibility. Normally, standing committees meet twice a week while the House of Commons is sitting (the Commons usually sits twenty-six weeks a year). On occasion, committees will meet more often or when the Commons is not sitting if the workload is heavy or a matter requires urgent attention. Generally, meetings are two hours long and are open to members of the public and the media.

An important power of a standing committee is reviewing and amending legislation sent to it from the House of Commons, usually after debate and adoption at second reading. It is here, in committee, that the legislation is reviewed in greater detail. Amendments are normally made while the legislation is in front of the committee. Once the committee has completed its review of the legislation, it proceeds to adopt the legislation clause by clause, making amendments as necessary. The legislation is then sent back to the Commons, where it begins the final debate, culminating in a vote.

Another important power of standing committees is the power to review, approve or reduce government spending (the parliamentary term for proposed spending is "estimates") for government departments within the committee's mandate. A committee may vote to reduce this spending but cannot vote to increase it. Standing committees also have the power to review appointments proposed or made by the government within their area of oversight. The committee may call the person to be appointed to review their qualifications and abilities. While the government retains the final right to decide the appointment, the committee can state whether it agrees with the government's decision.

Yet another important power of standing committees is the power to issue reports reflecting the views of their members by majority vote. These reports are tabled in the House by the committee chair, at which point they become public documents. There is no limit on the number of reports a committee can issue; they may be as short as one page or run hundreds of pages. The issuance of reports on issues that fall within the committee's mandate occupies the bulk of the work for most standing committees.

Members of a Standing Committee

The process to determine committee membership starts at the beginning of a new Parliament, after every election, with the establishment of the Standing Committee on Procedure and House Affairs. This standing committee delegates the decisions regarding which MPs will sit on standing committees to the party whips. Each whip, working closely with the party leader's office, decides which of their MPs will be appointed to fill their seat allocations on the committees.

This is not the end of the party leader's control of committee membership. At any time, party whips can substitute a different caucus member for a regular member. The standing orders allow whips to initiate a substitution simply by providing a written notice to the committee clerk. While the substitution is in effect only for the day on which notice is given, there is no limit to the number of notices that the party whip can provide. In some cases, the use of substitution is due to nothing more than a committee member's scheduling conflict. In other cases it is used to control proceedings by inserting a more compliant substitute. Party whips can also change membership of a standing committee via the tabling of a new report of the Standing Committee on Procedure and House Affairs in the House of Commons. This is used (less frequently) when permanent change in committee membership is desired.

Chair of a Standing Committee

The chair of a standing committee plays an important role. In 2016, the position came with remuneration of $11,165 per year. While committee members make decisions on general direction, committee chairs make the day-to-day decisions about that work. Committee meetings occur at the call of the chair, and committees cannot meet without the presence of a chair. Committee chairs preside over meetings, determining who gets to speak and maintaining order and decorum. On any question regarding procedure, the chair makes the determination on how to proceed. Committee chairs are also responsible for calling witnesses, both individuals and groups, to testify and provide evidence.

The chair does not move motions; that is the purview of the other members of the committee. The chair does not vote except in two situations: when a committee is considering a private bill (an extremely rare occurrence), the chair may vote along with other committee members; or when there is a tie, the chair casts the tie-breaking vote. Committee chairs also direct the staff of a committee, which normally consists of a clerk and one or more research analysts. They also submit operational budgets to the liaison committee for approval and manage these budgets once approved.

Committee chairs also represent the committee when tabling committee reports in the House of Commons and act as the main spokesperson for the committee through the media or Question Period. From time to time they also welcome and host official delegations from other legislatures, particularly when those delegations have an interest in the work of the committee.

The Selection of Committee Chairs

While committee chairs are technically elected by committee members, in effect they are appointed. Twenty of the chairs are appointed by the prime minister and four by the leader of the official Opposition. When committees meet for the first time at the beginning of each session of Parliament, their only business is the election of a chair. To be eligible to run for election as chair, members must meet two requirements. First, the member must be a regular member of the committee. Second, the member must be a member of a particular recognized party specified in the standing orders for the position of chair. For twenty out of the twenty-four committees, the standing orders require that the chair be a member of the party in government. Members of the party in official Opposition chair the remaining four committees: Public Accounts; Status of Women; Access to Information, Privacy and Ethics; and Government Operations and Estimates.

At first glance committee chairs are freely elected by committee members. However, it is almost unheard of for a committee to conduct an election of chair, because it is rare that more than one committee member is nominated for election. The party whips control who gets nominated, disciplining any member who nominates someone not chosen by the whip and leader. The election of chair at a committee's first meeting is merely a perfunctory formality.

The Problem with Standing Committees

In theory, standing committees have immense power to hold the government to account, such as the right to call witnesses, demand evidence and issue reports. In practice, they often do not exercise these rights for the reason that party leaders exert substantial control over the chairs and membership of these committees. In a majority Parliament, at least six out of ten members of a standing committee are appointed through the party whip by the prime minister. This means that part of the executive branch of government, the Prime Minister's Office (PMO), effectively controls a standing committee of the legislative branch. This is at complete odds with the fundamental role of a committee of the legislature, which is to hold the executive branch of government to account.

Committee reports are a good example of how the PMO exerts control over committees. Parliamentary secretaries, who work closely with the minister's office, sit on committees. When a draft report is being considered, the report is often sent to the minister's office through the parliamentary secretary. This means the minister's office is often participating in drafting the very reports that are supposed to hold the minister and department to account. This is putting the fox in charge of the henhouse. Ministers and departments also avoid accountability through the power the PMO exerts by instructing government caucus members not to support the calling of a minister or departmental official, or not to support the production of evidence.

Few amendments are ever made in committee to improve government legislation. In the Canadian House of Commons, amendments made to government bills by standing committees in any given year usually number in the single digits. In contrast, government bills in the British House of Commons are amended dozens if not hundreds of times in any given year. Furthermore, committees often do not review and approve government spending. In the event a committee does nothing with the estimates sent to it by the Commons within a certain time frame, the estimates are deemed automatically approved and reported back to the Commons. It is far more convenient for government to have estimates automatically reported back to the Commons than to have the committee review, critique and possibly reduce government spending.

It is unheard of in the Canadian system for the first minister, the prime minister, to be called before committee to be held to account. This is not true in the British parliament, where the prime minister is regularly called in front of the liaison committee to be held accountable by the chairs of the various committees. Since July 16, 2002, the British prime minister has appeared twice a year at liaison committee to be questioned on the government's domestic and international policies.

Another challenge is that the number of standing committees has increased significantly in recent years, occupying a lot of time for a typical member—not all of it productive. During a regular two-hour committee, a member typically gets no more than ten minutes, often just five minutes, to ask questions and provide comment. Since a committee normally meets twice a week, this means many members sit through four hours of committee to participate for as little as ten minutes. While there is no doubt utility in listening to the testimony of witnesses and questions and comments from other members of the committee, this is an enormous amount of time to spend waiting to participate. MPs who sit on two committees typically spend eight hours a week in committee, participating for as little as twenty minutes. This time does not include preparation time, such as reading briefs prepared by analysts or preparing questions to ask of witnesses.

Committee Reform in the UK

It is useful to look at recent reforms to the select committees of the UK House of Commons when considering reforms to standing committees of the Canadian House of Commons. (Select committees are the UK equivalent of standing committees in Canada.) Until 2010, select committees elected their chairs in a manner similar to that of Canadian standing committees, with committee chairs insufficiently independent of party leaders and the prime minister. Owing to the work of the Reform of the House of Commons Committee, a number of changes were made to select committees. Informally named the Wright Committee after its chair, MP Tony Wright, the committee recommended that chairs be elected by the House via secret preferential ballot and that committee members be elected by their party caucuses. These recommendations were agreed to by the incoming coalition government made up of Conservatives and Liberal Democrats.

As a result, most select committee chairs are now directly elected by the House of Commons. As in Canada, select committee chairs are reserved for a particular recognized party; unlike Canada, chair positions are reserved in proportion to the recognized parties' standings in the Commons, with more chairs allocated to opposition parties. All MPs vote for candidates for committee chair, and not just for the chair positions allocated to their party. Chairs may only be removed if their committees pass a motion of non-confidence in the chair. However, there are also term limits for chairs, consisting of two parliaments or eight years, whichever is longer.

The UK method of electing chairs increases the independence of the chairs and committees from party leaders, particularly the prime minister. However, it has also meant that the chair is less answerable to the committee members than if the chair had been directly elected by them. The other change made to select committees was that committee members are elected by party caucuses through secret ballots. Once each party has completed its internal elections for these positions (which can take up to a month to conduct), the Commons as a whole agrees to the membership of committees and the members are appointed for an entire parliament; membership can change, but those changes must be confirmed by the Commons as a whole.

While it has been only a few years since the implementation of these changes (not a long time for an institution that has been around for nearly one thousand years!), several observations can be made. First, UK committees seem to be taken more seriously by the government and there is increased government accountability to committees. Chairs of select committees have a higher profile, as result of being elected by the Commons and being seen as a source of alternative viewpoints to those of the government. Committee reports are more regularly referenced in House debates than before the changes and there is stronger financial scrutiny of government spending by committees.

A more specific example worth examination is the UK committee that oversees national security and intelligence-gathering activities. The Intelligence and Security Committee (ISC) was created in 1994 and initially operated under direct control of the prime minister. In 2013, legislation expanded its powers and made it independent of the prime minister. Under these changes, the prime minister nominates candidates for the committee, but both houses of Parliament (Commons and Lords) must confirm their respective parliamentarians. The chair is elected by committee members at the first meeting of the committee. As a result, the ISC has greater autonomy and a greater ability to hold government to account.

A Canadian Attempt at Reform
In Canada, the Security Intelligence Review Committee (SIRC) has traditionally performed the role of overseeing the government's national security and intelligence-gathering activities. The committee was established in 1984 and is made up of five members appointed by the prime minister. While SIRC reports to Parliament, it is not a committee of Parliament. SIRC has been criticized for not being independent enough to hold the government accountable, especially in light of the recent passage of legislation giving government greater powers to surveil its citizens. In response the government introduced legislation, Bill C-22, to establish a new National Security and Intelligence Committee (NSIC). Introduced in 2016, the bill proposes a joint committee made up of nine members: seven from the Commons and two from the Senate, with ministers and parliamentary secretaries being ineligible.

Members of the committee would be appointed by the prime minister and serve at the pleasure of the prime minister. The prime minister would also appoint the committee chair. While the committee is made up of parliamentarians, unlike the UK's ISC it is not a committee of Parliament; it would report directly to the prime minister. Ministers will have the power to terminate the committee's review of operations and be allowed to withhold information on "national security" grounds. Finally, the bill allows the prime minister to review committee reports and require revisions before they are finalized and made public.

All this makes the committee self-defeating. The purpose of the committee is to hold the government accountable for its national security and intelligence-gathering activities. Since the committee members serve at the pleasure of the prime minister, it is difficult to see how they could possibly hold government to account. Reporting to the prime minister rather than to the House further weakens accountability, as does the power of the prime minister to review draft reports and require revisions.

Real Reform of Standing Committees

The ultimate goal of committee reform should be to better hold government to account. Canadians do not elect governments, they elect legislatures. The government is formed out of a group of MPs in the elected House of Commons, and the MP with the support of the majority is the person appointed prime minister by the Governor General. The prime minister in turn selects the MPs who will serve in cabinet. As a result, it is essential that the elected legislature be able to hold this unelected executive to account. Committees should be feared by the PMO rather than controlled by the PMO.

The first reform that should be contemplated is removing the party whip's power to appoint committee members and giving it to elected MPs on a secret preferential ballot vote, just as the Speaker is elected. These elections could take place after the Speaker is elected, and the elections could be administered within each party caucus. Regardless of the time and place of these elections, it is essential that they be by secret ballot and through a democratic process where party leaders cannot control who is nominated.

The second reform that should be pursued is the allocation of committee chairs. Chairs should be allocated in proportion to their party standings in the Commons. In the Parliament elected in 2015, this would entail fourteen chairs for the Liberals, seven chairs for the Conservatives and three chairs for the New Democrats, rather than the current standings of twenty chairs for the Liberals and four chairs for the Conservatives.

The third reform that should be considered is the true election of committee chairs. Chairs should be directly accountable to the committee itself and should be elected by secret ballot. In order to ensure that party whips cannot control the system as they do now (by disciplining party members who nominate a candidate other than the one chosen by the whip and party leader), every committee member's name should appear on the ballot. A single preferential ballot (rather than multiple ballots) could be used for efficiency of time, while ensuring the chair has the support of the majority of committee members. This system would ensure that the chair is truly democratically elected and accountable to the committee members rather than to the PMO or party leader.

Another reform would be to amend the standing orders to remove the "automatically deemed reported" rule for estimates. Committees should be required to review, critique and vote on proposed government spending. This, after all, is a fundamental reason for the existence of Parliament: that government spending and taxation must only occur with the consent of the people's elected representatives.

Finally, the number of standing committees should be reduced by merging committees that share similar mandates. This would free up time and resources for the several dozen MPs who do double duty on committees and allow them to focus on a single committee. Eliminating just five committees would ensure that no member is required to do double duty.

Conclusion

Compared to other established democracies, Canadian party leaders have much more power to control MPs. The real power of the House of Commons is held by only a few elected MPs, particularly the prime minister and other party leaders. Greater freedom from party-leader power is needed for elected MPs to fulfill their constitutional role in holding government to account. These reforms proposed to standing committees are not just nice to have, but critical in ensuring checks and balances on executive power between general elections. Since the elected MP is the people's only elected representative at the national level, strengthening that role will strengthen public confidence in our democratic institutions. The decline of the power of elected MPs since Confederation is the result of many changes made to our parliamentary system over the years. There is no reason why future changes cannot restore balance. All that is required is political will to make these improvements and an acknowledgement, especially on the part of party leaders, of the excessive concentration of power.

Bibliography

Beauchesne, Arthur. *Beauchesne's Parliamentary Rules and Forms*, 3rd ed. (Toronto: Canada Law Book Company, 1943).

Mottram, Sir Richard, Roger Dawe, Peter Facey, Alexandra Runswick and Professor Patrick Dunleavy. Oral evidence given to the Political and Constitutional Reform Committee of the UK House of Commons on the committee study "Revisiting *Rebuilding the House*: The Impact of the Wright Reforms" (London: UK Parliament, April 18, 2013), http://www.publications.parliament.uk/pa/cm201213/cmselect/cmpolcon/uc1062-iii/uc106201.htm.

O'Brien, Audrey and Marc Bosc. *House of Commons Procedure and Practice*, 2nd ed. (Ottawa: Thomson Reuters, 2009).

Rogers, Robert and Rhodri Walters. *How Parliament Works*, 7th ed. (Abingdon, Oxon: Routledge, 2015).

Speaking in Parliament

Nathan Cullen

The impression most new MPs get when they rise to make their so-called "maiden speech" in Parliament is that no one is actually listening. One would imagine that at this important moment, this virginal step into the official record of such a hallowed place, the new MP would be joined by a suitably large group of other members. They would assemble around the new MP in just the right formation for the television cameras to capture their interested and nodding faces. They would applaud even if the new MP, often nervous and almost inevitably reading from some overworked script, only allowed them a moment or two in that first flight of oratory.

I failed miserably in my first effort.

I had been given a speech by my newly hired legislative assistant only minutes before (procrastination and last-minute brilliance would be the calling cards of our office for years to come). My new legislative assistant had been told by sage colleagues that part of his job was to write speeches for the boss—never mind that I hadn't used a single speech in the campaign that had got me into Parliament in the first place. The whole thing had been quite a panic. With only half an hour's notice that I would be making my historic speech (and only one shot at first impressions) we had rushed together as a team, my staff typing furiously, me literally running across the lawn of Parliament Hill to make the clock.

I had been told by my equally experienced colleagues that I was to read my speech like a dutiful and respectable politician. If I could muster a little authentic emotion at various points in the delivery that would be appreciated by my grand audience, but it wasn't necessarily expected on this first lap around the track. I believe I might have made it through the first or maybe second minute of what I'm sure was a very fine piece of speech writing when I couldn't stomach it much more. I was bored, and I assumed my audience must have been equally so.

As I set the paper down firmly on the wooden lectern that had been so helpfully provided by a parliamentary page about a decade my junior, I felt as if I were launching my canoe onto an unknown river. More out of desperation than according to any great plan, I began to speak from my heart what little information my head could offer. Lacking in the latter, I chose to rely heavily on the former. And other than the technically draining procedural rants of a house leader and the stress-filled content of Question Period attacks, ranging in length from twenty-five-second to the very dangerous thirty-five-second questions, I have never again read a speech in Parliament. It is, as you might expect, a small point of personal pride.

I have been told of a British tradition in their parliament, the "mother of all parliaments" (as if we were birthed whole from that ancient building and now wander the planet as miscreant children), that if a member began reading from a prepared text, other MPs present were meant to shout out "Paper!" as loud as they might until the person stopped. While I won't give the British much credit for creativity, I will suggest that they're on to something.

It might seem a trivial notion but I would suggest that bringing such a tradition to our Parliament might restore some of the respect the place once enjoyed, press those elected to speak on our behalf to know something of which they speak, and cut the umbilical cord to the backrooms and political staff, whose purposes are not always aligned with those of a good representative. If there is anything that recent political upheavals have taught me (Brexit, Trump, etc.) it is that the citizen will now place authenticity and an attempt at reflecting sincere sentiment, however dangerous, over any politically correct, careful and ultimately cynical attempt at politics—"Take your focus groups, polling and targeted messaging and shove it!"

I may be placing too much importance on this one aspect of our Parliament, but there are reforms that come along from time to time that seem small and trivial, yet carry the significant impact of restoring or even renewing something we thought was lost. The connection between the elected and the electors needs such restoration. So does the belief that dialogue, sincere and unscripted, is the only way people ever work through problems.

Words matter. We might not always appreciate this, and the general cynicism and skepticism political speeches are viewed with today might seem to diminish this truth. Yet one fact remains: we have all been moved to action, drawn into deep emotion and brought to a new understanding through the words spoken by others. Why should we expect so little from speeches made in our central institution and from those whose talents and ambition have brought them there to work?

I attended a naming feast in Kitamaat Village in northwestern BC some years ago at the invitation of a friend. The Haisla tradition of naming is sacred, careful and an honour to bear witness to. My friend's daughter, all of six years of age, was getting a name along with several other Haisla of varying ages and statures. As a people raise themselves in the community through good acts and attention to tradition, they may receive increasingly important names that carry with them increasing power and responsibility.

The person receiving the name is also meant to incorporate the best qualities of the people who held that name before. Stories are told sometimes going back centuries of deeds and accomplishments that those people performed for the nation. The stories are repeated again and again to build the force of that name and emphasize the obligation of the new name-bearer to bring no shame to the stories.

Toward the end of the seven-hour-long ceremony, an elder slowly made his way to the microphone at the front of the gym. Under banners celebrating basketball championships, in front of the bleachers, he slowly began to talk in Haisla. After a short while people began to come out of the stands—men, women, whole families—to stand behind him, silently and respectfully. The longer he spoke the larger the crowd grew, and soon well over a hundred Haisla stood behind him.

Not understanding the Haisla language or the meaning of what I was seeing, I sought my friend out and quietly asked if she might interpret the words and the gesture. "Oh, this is one of our oldest and most important actions. He is the head of their house and speaks for them. They stand behind him as if to say, 'His words are our words. His promises are ours.' In older times this was how declarations of war and the making of peace were done—by our leaders with the actual backing of the people.".

Only days later, I stood in Parliament and retold this story. I had asked permission of my Haisla friends to tell other Canadians about what I had seen and they had agreed. I asked the Canadian House to imagine if every time we stood to speak on behalf of our constituents, we could feel a similar weight of responsibility. Imagine if we held in our minds those that have gone before and brought respect and dignity to their work. Imagine how our speeches would be changed. Imagine how Question Period would look! In our short-attention-span, Donald Trump–filled world of politics, the temptations are great to consider the next headline, the next "like" and the next retweet as our only measures of effectiveness. We're given little to no encouragement to dignify ourselves, to reach for a higher purpose and use words we know our fellow citizens might also use.

Throughout my career I've been happily surprised to realize that the speeches I cared most about, talking about issues critical to the progress of our country, are those that I hear about most. These speeches are often between ten and twenty minutes long, far beyond what the social media experts tell us is a useful length. Yet it is through social media that people come to see what politicians are saying—and while I like a good, shareable political cartoon or quote as much as the next person, I too feel the need for something more. It's the difference between reading a great news or magazine article and reading a great book. Both have their place, but in the introduction of the new we shouldn't completely abandon what we love about the old.

Breaking the Parliamentary Glass Ceiling

Anita Vandenbeld

Introduction

In most spheres of life, women in Canada have achieved significant levels of equality. While they are breaking glass ceilings in educational attainment, business, law and other professions, one exception is political participation. According to the Inter-Parliamentary Union, in September 2016 Canada ranked sixty-fourth in the world in terms of the number of women elected to Parliament, behind countries such as South Sudan (sixty-first), Afghanistan (fifty-second), Uganda (thirty-first) and Rwanda (first).[94] Why is a country that considers itself to be a global leader in equality, rights and economic participation of women lagging so far behind on women in political leadership? What are the structural barriers that prevent women from being elected in the first place? How are these inequalities perpetuated within the functioning of Parliament to cause female MPs to have higher attrition rates than their male counterparts? As a first-term female MP who was elected in 2015 and also ran in the 2011 election and has worked around the world managing a global network to encourage women's political participation, I will attempt to deconstruct what is causing this inequality and how we can make changes to improve in the future.

---

94. Inter-Parliamentary Union's Women in National Parliaments database: http://www.ipu.org/wmn-e/classif.htm.

Many solutions have been proposed over the years, including quotas, electoral reform, parliamentary reforms and political financing reforms. I will argue that the greatest barriers to electing more women in Canada are these: political-party nomination processes, pervading stereotypes and negative attacks, and a sense of "limited space" that prevents women from working together to achieve transformative change. Changing the rules under which parties select candidates and providing more opportunities for cross-party cooperation within Parliament, such as an all-party women's caucus, can help Canada to achieve the critical mass and cultural shift needed to break down the "old boys' networks" and social bias that discourage women from entering and remaining in politics.

The Problem

Throughout 150 years of history, only 314 women have ever had the privilege of being elected to Canada's House of Commons. Today only 26 percent of the seats in the House of Commons are held by women, an increase of just 8 percentage points over the past twenty years. One woman has been prime minister (albeit only for five months) and only three women have been the leader of the official Opposition (all of them either acting or interim leaders).

It was once assumed that the lack of women in elected office was due to there being fewer women with the educational or professional qualifications and experience in the "pipeline." However according to the World Economic Forum, Canada is ranked first in the world in women's educational attainment; first in parity of professional and technical workers; sixteenth in income parity; and twenty-third in women's labour-force participation. When it comes to political empowerment we are ranked forty-sixth.[95] This means there are other factors that need to be examined to determine why Canadian women are not participating equally in politics.

With the bold decision by Prime Minister Justin Trudeau to appoint a gender-equal cabinet in 2015, Canada catapulted into a leadership position globally for the number of female ministers—but this in some ways glosses over structural barriers that still remain. While having 50 percent women in cabinet—from diverse backgrounds—has had

---

95. World Economic Forum, *The Global Gender Gap Report 2015*.

extraordinary positive impacts on creating positive role models for women, changing our view of what a political leader looks and sounds like, and enhancing women's voices and perspectives at the decision-making table, it has also highlighted the barriers and prejudices that women face. Female ministers are heckled more often and more loudly. Women are held to higher ethical standards and are therefore subject to attack. And feminine leadership characteristics—such as compassion, listening and cooperation—are commonly perceived as signs of weakness. Gender parity in cabinet has also highlighted the double standard for women who are mothers—if they take time for their families they are criticized, but if they do not they are attacked for being "bad mothers." Much of the current dialogue—and in some cases backlash—against women as political leaders in Canada is an unintended consequence of having more women in cabinet; whether it becomes a beachhead or leads to regression depends on how we respond at this moment in history.

As soon as we move beyond the cabinet, we see very little has changed for women in politics in Canada. One hundred years after the first women got the right to vote, we have not achieved even close to parity. The first woman elected to Parliament was Agnes Macphail in 1921. But progress was slow. By 1988 there were still only 13.3 percent women in the House of Commons. This grew to 18 percent in 1993 and then stagnated between 20 and 22 percent until 2011, when 24.7 percent women were elected.[96] The 2015 election, which was heavily lauded as having achieved the highest number of women ever elected in Canada, was actually only a 1.3 percentage point increase. At other levels of government it is similar: in 2014 the average number of women in provincial legislatures was 21.4 percent and among municipal councillors it was 26 percent. While there have been several female premiers elected, the number of mayors is still only 16 percent.[97]

Background

A recent poll in Canada asked the public why it thought women were under-represented in politics. Reasons given ranged from lack of support from political parties (40 percent), family commitments

---

96. Parliament of Canada website.
97. "Fundamental Facts: Elected Women in Canada by the Numbers," *Equal Voice*, June 2014.

(38 percent), higher standards placed on women, and the negative tone/mudslinging of politics (23 percent).[98] These results are consistent with my own experience. From 2008 to 2010, I was the global project manager of the International Knowledge Network of Women in Politics (iKNOW Politics), a technology-based peer support network that promotes women in politics on five continents, operating in four languages. I have run women's campaign colleges and provided technical support to women's caucuses and committees in several countries, including Haiti, the Democratic Republic of the Congo, Kosovo and Bangladesh. I first ran (successfully) in a very competitive nomination in 2010. I was a candidate in the 2011 federal election running against a senior cabinet minister. I ran again in a competitive nomination in 2014 and I was elected in 2015. During this time I participated in national peer-support calls with other female Liberal candidates led by a female Liberal MP, and since being elected I have taken over leadership of these biweekly calls with the women who planned to run in 2015. I am also the chair of the Liberal women's caucus and the all-party parliamentary women's caucus. In all of these capacities I have worked with thousands of women candidates and elected representatives. Although each story is different, it is remarkable to me how many of the same themes repeat themselves regardless of region, culture or political affiliation.

Political Parties and Nomination Processes
Around the world, women identify the selection processes of political parties as one of the most significant barriers to entering politics. The same is true in Canada. The reason women are not getting elected in Canada is not because Canadians do not vote for women. In fact statistically, women are elected in proportion to the number of women who are nominated by their parties—or in even higher numbers.[99] Political scientist Melanee Thomas, referring to a 2013 study, has stated, "We can find no evidence that voters discriminate against women candidates. We did find considerable evidence that party [nomination committees] were

---

98. Éric Grenier, "Canadians Feel Men Have Easier Time in Politics, but Women Have the Chops, Poll Suggests," CBC News, July 25, 2016.
99. "Number of Women Candidates a Paltry 24%," *Equal Voice*, May 2005.

more likely to discriminate against women candidates."[100] The problem for women appears to be getting on the ballot in the first place. This means encouraging more women to run, and making sure that parties nominate them.

Florence Bird's 1967 Royal Commission on the Status of Women identified "a number of impediments to women seeking candidature; in particular prejudice in the constituency associations, inadequate financial resources and limited mobility...Women who have been successful at the polls confirm that winning the nomination is a more formidable hurdle than winning the election."[101] From the many peer-support calls I have participated in over the past six years, I can say anecdotally that this is as true today as it was then.

Women continue to be nominated in lower numbers than men. In the 2015 election there were more women candidates than ever before—533 women on the ballot—but that still accounts for only 30 percent of the candidates.[102] In addition, women continue to run in ridings that are less winnable than men's. According to one study, 59 percent of women ran in an opposing party's stronghold compared with 47 percent of men. Inversely, only 17 percent of women candidates ran in a riding considered to be a stronghold of their own party as opposed to 25 percent of men.[103] The inequality is perpetuated by the fact that most incumbents in winnable ridings are men.

Some say the reason women aren't winning is that they aren't running in the first place. While there is a need for more research on how many women consider running and don't, or drop out halfway through, there is ample evidence that there are fewer women "aspirants" than there are male ones. A 2014 Abacus online survey of 1,850 Canadians showed that only 15 percent of women said they were inclined to run for office, compared with 28 percent of men.[104] This mirrors similar studies

---

100. "50% population, 25% representation: Why the Parliamentary Gender Gap?" CBC News, cbc.ca/news2/interactives/women-politics, accessed September 24, 2016.

101. *Report of the Royal Commission on the Status of Women in Canada* (1970): 349.

102. Leslie Young, "By the Numbers: Women in Parliament," Global News, January 28, 2016.

103. Shannon Proudfoot, "Women in Politics: We're Not as Equal as We Think We Are," *Maclean's*, July 31, 2016.

104. "50% population, 25% representation," CBC News.

in the United States that point to an "ambition gap." Young girls are less likely than boys to have a parent or teacher talk to them about politics, and women are only half as likely to have someone make a suggestion that they should run for office.[105] Political parties are aware of this and have made significant efforts to recruit more women, as has Equal Voice, a multi-partisan organization dedicated to electing more women through social media campaigns encouraging citizens to ask a talented woman to run, campaigns to raise awareness among young women, and direct recruitment efforts. However, the gap persists.

One reason for this could be the nature of the nomination process itself. When voters are choosing a candidate in a general election, they ask themselves the questions: "Who reflects my values? Who do I trust? Who would best represent me?" The answers are just as likely to be a female candidate as a male one. But party members voting for a nomination contestant are asking a different question: "Who do I believe *other people* will want to vote for?" In doing so, they rely on who has won in the past: typically older, white males in high-level positions with name recognition—the so-called "star" candidates. By assessing a candidate's "winnability" as opposed to qualifications, party members introduce societal stereotypes and assumptions that may not actually be true. In fact a recent study shows that while 80 percent of Canadians believe both sexes make good political leaders, 85 percent of people believe that *others* think men make better leaders. And 59 percent agreed that it is "easier for men to get elected to high political office."[106] And so, party members nominate men in the erroneous hope that they will get more support from the public.

This bias toward "star" candidates who come from professions that are already over-represented by men (mayors, business leaders, media personalities, military leaders) over hard-working local community-builders, who are more likely to be women (school trustees, non-profit organization leaders, activists), is perpetuated by the party leadership in many cases. Parties will actively recruit high-profile candidates and "parachute" them into a riding even when there has been a female candidate working for years to build community relationships and who may have sacrificed time from her own career to dedicate it

---

105. Jennifer L. Lawless and Richard L. Fox, *It Still Takes a Candidate: Why Women Don't Run for Office* (Cambridge, UK: Cambridge University Press, 2010).

106. Grenier, "Canadians Feel Men Have Easier Time in Politics."

to running and building an election team and organization. Political parties interfere in local nomination contests in many ways, such as direct appointments by the party leader, manipulation of the vetting "greenlight" process, pressure on candidates to step aside for the "good" of the party, unequal enforcement of rules, or manipulation of the date and location of the nomination meetings.

In my own case, I left my job with the UN in April 2010 in order to run for a nomination in my home riding, which I was told would happen imminently. But the nomination meeting was delayed for seven months while party officials waited for an answer from a high-profile male candidate whom they were trying to recruit and whom they were offering an appointment. I learned recently from this person that he had been courted by not only the party leader but also a former prime minister. It was only after he ultimately declined the appointment that the nomination meeting was finally called and I won it easily.

I was very pleased that when Justin Trudeau became leader of the Liberal Party he immediately announced that he would not use his power of appointment. After my experience in 2010, if he had not made this commitment, I would almost certainly not have run again. The possibility of putting all one's time and energy and financial resources into a contest only to be bumped by an "appointment" is demoralizing and unfair. It is a story I have heard time and again from women candidates. Even though this power of appointment was ostensibly put in place to ensure that more women ran, I believe it has done more to deter women than to encourage them. All too often women are encouraged to run when a riding looks unwinnable, so they work at it for years raising money and building relationships to turn it into a winnable riding—and then they become a victim of their own success as parties court a big-name man once it looks like it can be won. Even when party leaders and senior officials have good intentions, too often the middle-level party officials and riding associations continue to play gatekeeper, further discouraging women from running.

Negative Politics, Stereotypes and Media Bias
Another deterrent to women choosing politics is how women are treated once elected. The lack of decorum during Question Period, the extreme partisanship and the way in which women are portrayed in the media turn many women away from politics. Women MPs are heckled

more loudly, receive more vulgar comments and face greater public scrutiny than their male counterparts. Their families are also pulled into the public sphere and mentioned more often in media articles than those of male politicians. Many women shy away out of concern for personal privacy for themselves and their families, especially their children.

Women are also criticized more for their appearance and other non-policy-related traits. When I first decided to run I sought out an experienced female former MP for advice. What she told me was, "Start wearing lipstick." This is another dilemma for women. I am criticized for not wearing high heels or skirts very often—I prefer pantsuits. And yet my female colleagues who do wear these things are criticized for being sexualized. All too often media coverage of a woman focuses on what she was wearing or how she looked rather than what she said. This kind of coverage tends to make women seem frivolous and lacking in policy ideas, which only exacerbates the popular stereotypes about women in politics. Women are also referred to in the media with qualifiers attached to their names, like "young" or "female." During the 2011 campaign, when I ran against John Baird, who is less than two years older than me, I was frequently referred to as "young female candidate," while he was referred to as "senior cabinet minister." A recent *Equal Voice* article cited research performed by University of Toronto professor Sylvia Bashevkin:

> Relentless social media attacks, an overwhelming workload and heightened public scrutiny that disproportionately regards the missteps of female politicians as "personal failings" and reflective of fundamental character flaws are some of the reasons women opt to stay away...Women in politics are subject to harsher evaluations by the media and as a result, end up appearing to fall short on each and every metric. The extra scrutiny not only makes life more difficult for women in politics, but distracts from their political contributions, capabilities and opinions.[107]

This trend toward sensational journalism and the search for the latest scandal is particularly hard on women. Too often the justification for

107. "How 'Gotcha Journalism' Intensifies Sexism in Politics," *Equal Voice*, August 29, 2016.

why we need more women in politics is articulated through an essentialist view of the characteristics of women. I have heard arguments that when there are more women in politics, there will be less corruption, the tone of debate will rise, and politics will become less partisan and more cooperative. While there are many cases where these outcomes have occurred with more women in a legislative body, the other side of this argument results in women being held to a higher ethical standard, sometimes an impossible one, so that when women make the same mistakes that men do in politics, they are criticized much more harshly for them.

It also means that women who are more ambitious, aggressive in tone and partisan face more hostility by the media and the public for going against expected societal norms. This has been referred to as "role entrapment." If a woman displays feminine characteristics she is seen as "soft" and vulnerable and not powerful, but if she behaves like a man she is criticized for subverting gender norms and failing to meet expectations of women to bring greater civility and morality into the political domain. This dilemma has been popularly articulated by American businesswoman Sheryl Sandberg in her book *Lean In*, in which she says, "Success and likeability are positively correlated for men and negatively for women. When a man is successful, he is liked by both men and women. When a woman is successful, people of both genders like her less." [108]

Violence Against Women in Politics

Sometimes the backlash against women subverting societal gender norms has an even darker side to it—and the inflammatory rhetoric, verbal abuse and criticism of women in politics can cross the line into physical threats and attacks. In my international work I saw violence against women in politics as a significant barrier. I have often stated publicly that I am fortunate that in Canada I do not face the same threats to and fears about my personal safety. But that is not to say that intimidation and fear for safety are absent for women in Canadian politics. We just rarely talk about it publicly. I was once followed home late at night from my constituency office by someone who blocked my driveway until

---

108. Sheryl Sandberg, *Lean In: Women, Work, and the Will to Lead* (New York: Knopf, 2013): 40.

I got on the phone to call my husband. We installed an alarm system in our house and I now keep it on whenever I am home alone.

I know a female colleague who was threatened on social media prior to a public town hall meeting. She decided to ask the local police to be present that evening, which drew even more attacks and criticism. At least one female MP has cancelled her Twitter account because of anonymous partisan "trolls" strategically directing angry and misleading information to her profile. During my first election campaign someone painted a target with crosshairs on my campaign signs. After British MP Jo Cox was murdered in June 2016, I believe there is no female politician who doesn't at least have it cross her mind to fear for her safety when someone gets loud or angry toward her in a public place. I have worked around the world in some of the most dangerous countries— including the Congo—and since becoming a public official have found myself falling back on my UN security training to be hyper-vigilant about my surroundings, to change my patterns and to be aware of the nearest exit in a way I never have before in Canada. Yet asking for help is seen as weakness, and most female MPs will not report threatening incidents either out of fear of ridicule or fear that the incidents will be made public and will escalate.

The yelling and heckling in Question Period and the inflammatory way in which the media—especially social media—talk about politicians is making this a growing problem that may not only deter women from running, but could lead to attrition among current sitting MPs. In the past few months I have heard several of my female colleagues muse aloud about "Is it worth it?" But if good people are driven out of politics by threats and bullying, we will lose more than just women's voices. We will be allowing a discourse that is increasingly hostile toward all politicians to become a self-fulfilling prophecy, leaving only the power-hungry and the thick-skinned to run for office. I do not believe that is what we want as a country.

Family Commitments

Despite efforts by many men to take on more family responsibilities, the fact remains that in Canada women continue to carry the greater burden of caregiving for both children and aging parents. Until recently, there were very few women with young children running for office. There were trailblazers like Sheila Copps, who was the first woman to have a baby while a sitting MP, but they were rare. Many women waited until their children were older—or chose not to have children—to focus on their political aspirations.

I know of a woman in 2011 who won her party's nomination and when she became pregnant before the election she offered to run a second time for the nomination in order to be "fair" to the party members. I have never heard of a man doing the same thing because his wife got pregnant. There is currently a female MP who frequently has her baby with her in the House of Commons and whose experience has highlighted the fact that Parliament is not a family-friendly environment. From unpredictable votes and work hours, to a lack of flexible child-care options, to shuttle buses that are not stroller-friendly, to the lack of space for nursing and many other limitations, it is not easy to be both a politician and a parent. In addition, many MPs travel for hours each week to get to Ottawa and are away from their families four or five nights each week. This can be very hard on MPs' personal lives, and there is a very high divorce rate among parliamentarians. This family impact is a serious deterrent to many prospective MPs, but especially to women.

The Procedure and House Affairs Committee recently initiated a study on how to achieve a family-friendly Parliament, which heard from many witnesses about how our Parliament could be improved. The committee made recommendations about a more predictable schedule (especially for votes), flexible child-care options, revisions to travel points to make it easier for families to be together, and a gender-sensitive safety audit of Parliament.[109] The study also heard from witnesses about eliminating Friday sittings, as many other legislatures have done, but did not come to a decision on this. If the House of Commons does not make changes that will encourage representation of younger women, or of young parents of either gender, Canadians will be missing an important voice in a decision-making process that should be reflecting a variety of life experiences.

---

109. Standing Committee on Procedure and House Affairs, "Initiatives Toward a Family-Friendly House of Commons," 42nd Parliament, 1st session, June 15, 2016, http://www.parl.gc.ca/Committees/en/PROC/StudyActivity?studyActivityId=8775954.

Money

Although Canada has relatively progressive spending limits and reporting requirements on nomination and election campaigns, money is still a deterrent for many women aspiring to politics. This is even more true for women with disabilities, indigenous women and visible minorities. The gendered wage gap in Canada is still seventy-three cents to the dollar, so women are not making as much money as their male counterparts. The lack of women in corporate boardrooms and as CEOs also means that fewer women have access to the money networks needed to fundraise for a political campaign. The increased length of political campaigns and the introduction of fixed election dates have resulted in an almost perma-campaign, which means that candidates who are not financially independent and who need to work for a living—many of them women—are at an increased disadvantage compared with those who can take long periods of time off from their careers to campaign full-time. And there are still significant gaps in our political party financing legislation.

There have been reforms over the years. In the early 2000s it was the Liberal women's caucus that pushed to have nomination campaigns included in the Chrétien government's political party financing legislation. This was a significant reform that helped to minimize one of the biggest barriers for women. Before that, there were no spending limits or restrictions on nomination contests, meaning that in a winnable riding the cost of running could be in the hundreds of thousands of dollars, with few rules or restrictions on how the money was raised or spent. However, the spending limits and reporting requirements apply only to a nomination contestant or to an electoral candidate. From the time a contestant is nominated to the drop of the writ (the calling of the election), that individual is no longer officially subject to the political financing laws (with some exceptions). This is a significant loophole that should be closed.

In addition, there has been very little enforcement and few punitive measures taken against candidates who violate the laws, either by political parties or by Elections Canada. The common practice of nomination contestants paying for memberships in their political party rarely results in any consequences even when it is reported to the parties. In the rare case that a candidate does get charged by Elections Canada, the process takes such a long time that they may have sat in Parliament for two terms before there are any consequences. This was the case with Dean Del Mastro, who was convicted in 2014 of falsifying documents and exceeding the spending limit during the 2008 election. He ran and won again in 2011 and sat in the House of Commons for six years before he was forced to resign. He spent only one month in jail and four months under house arrest.

Throughout the women's candidate calls I have participated in for years, the common complaint is that especially for nomination campaigns, the rules are opaque, the process is not transparent and political parties are more concerned with hiding potential bad news stories than with enforcing rules. Although there are women who abuse the system as well, the greatest challenge I have heard women discuss on the calls is the fact that they want to follow the rules while nobody else does. As long as there is little enforcement of financial reporting rules and spending limits, women will continue to be disadvantaged in both nomination and election campaigns.

The 2015 election was the longest—and most expensive—in more than one hundred years. Since the spending limits depend on the number of days in the campaign, this resulted in much higher limits than in previous elections. In addition, the introduction of fixed election dates means candidates know years in advance what the date of the election will be. This has resulted in a de facto lengthening of the campaign period similar to what happens in the United States. Whereas most candidates previously worked full-time until the moment the writ dropped—because they did not know when that might happen—now there is an increasing trend toward candidates taking leaves of absence from their jobs for much longer. This again disadvantages less wealthy candidates, many of them women.

Women in Parliament
Even after women make it past all the hurdles and get elected to Parliament, they continue to face greater barriers than men. One of these barriers is in what portfolios and assignments women MPs are given compared with men. Women are often given "soft" portfolios such as health, labour, international development, heritage and status of women. There has never been a female minister of finance or minister of agriculture, and since 1867 there has only ever been one woman as minister of defence (Kim Campbell) and one solicitor general/minister

of public safety (Anne McLellan). Similarly, a recent *Globe and Mail* article indicated that committee assignments were made on a gendered basis. Two of the twenty-four committees currently have not a single woman on them. Seven of them have only one woman. And yet the Standing Committee on the Status of Women had nine women and just one man.[110] This was recently addressed with the addition of one more man on the committee; however the imbalance remains. Women in Parliament still largely occupy the spaces in the so-called "women's issues," whether by choice or because that is the space that is most readily open to them.

Women also tend to view the space that is open to them as being extremely narrow compared with men. This sometimes prevents women from working together to overcome barriers—they see one another as competitors for a limited number of positions rather than allies. For example, if a woman looks at a coveted committee and sees only one woman on it, she might say to herself, "I want to be that one woman," and she may work against other women who have a similar interest. Men, on the other hand, see nine possible openings and don't feel the same sense of competitiveness. This concept of limited space for women works against the ability of women to achieve "critical mass." Critical mass theory originated with Drude Dahlerup in the 1980s and soon became prevalent in the United Nations and other organizations that were promoting women in politics. It held that when a legislative body became 30 percent women, a tipping point would be reached and transformative change would occur.

Recently it has been recognized that this critical mass depends on the ability of women to create supportive alliances. For example, legislatures with strong women's caucuses, or where feminist men are also included, can mimic critical mass even with smaller numbers. And those where women (and men) do not form alliances or do not identify with a feminist consciousness may not reach critical mass no matter how many women are elected.[111] This suggests that to break the glass ceilings that still exist for women in Parliament, it is not enough to elect

---

110. Jane Taber, "Canada Has More Women in Cabinet, But Fewer Sit on Commons Committees," *Globe and Mail*, March 8, 2016.

111. Sarah Childs and Mona Lena Krook, "Critical Mass Theory and Women's Political Representation," *Political Studies* 56 (2008): 725–36.

more women. Women and men need to consciously work together to eliminate the barriers.

Proposed Policy Options

There is no shortage of literature and comparative practice regarding solutions to electing more women. The network I used to manage—iKNOW Politics—has an entire library of literature and knowledge products on this topic. Canadian organizations such as Equal Voice actively advocate for reforms to elect more women.

Quotas

The most common solution used internationally is to establish quotas for women. There are 112 countries with voluntary quotas and 54 with legislated quotas.[112] The use of such quotas is mapped internationally on a website called quotaproject.org. It indicates the two occasions on which Canadian political parties have had voluntary quotas. The first was in 1985, when the NDP set a quota of 50 percent women candidates; the second was in 1993, when the Liberal Party set a quota of 25 percent female candidates. It also indicates that the NDP does not allow a nomination contest to go ahead without at least one woman running, which is a form of quota. Other parties have set targets in recent years—typically around 30 percent—but these were not formalized.

The success rate of quotas depends on the type of electoral system, local political culture and level of enforcement. For example, among the fifty-four countries with mandatory legislated quotas the average number of women elected is 24.9 percent, but this ranges from 2 percent (Solomon Islands) to 53 percent (Bolivia). Electing more women takes much more than simply legislating it.

Voluntary party quotas have been successful in countries with proportional representation with closed party lists, but these also increase the power of political parties to select candidates. In first-past-the-post systems there are limited means to enforce voluntary quotas. Direct appointment of candidates can deter many qualified women from running and undermines the autonomy of local communities in choosing their candidate. In the United Kingdom, the Labour Party has certain seats set aside for women-only candidate lists. And some

---

112. All statistics in this paragraph were deduced from information at QuotaProject.org.

have proposed that each constituency elect two MPs—one man and one woman.

Some countries have introduced reserved seats for women either appointed from civil society (Rwanda) or elected by Parliament (Bangladesh). However, these indirectly elected MPs are often seen as lacking legitimacy and are therefore less influential. And countries that have reserved seats elect only 20.8 percent women—below the global average.

In Canada it is commonly held that quotas—or affirmative action—go against the merit principle and are undemocratic. However, quotas have existed in our political system for a long time. In fact, I am a product of a quota. When I was a teenager, I joined the Liberal Party to support a friend who was running for a position. I probably would have quickly lost interest, except that the party was having a provincial leadership race and there was a requirement that the slate of delegates from every constituency include at least four young people, of whom two had to be female. Given that there were very few young women joining the Liberal Party in Calgary in the 1980s, I became sought-after as a delegate and was invited to meet some of the leadership candidates personally. This sparked my interest in politics, and it is quite likely that without the quota I would not be where I am today.

Electoral Reform

At the time of this book's publication, Canada was in the midst of a national dialogue about its electoral system. Regarding women in politics, first-past-the-post (FPTP) systems elect the fewest women. In fact, the bottom ten countries in the world for the number of women elected all have FPTP systems. Countries with proportional representation (PR) and mixed member proportional (MMP) electoral systems tend to elect, on average, twice as many women (24 percent) as FPTP (12 percent). However this depends greatly on the type of PR system—the range is as broad as the number of different systems that exist.

Political Financing Reforms

There is a gendered element to campaign financing that has been documented for many years. Women in Canada tend to outspend their male counterparts by 10 percent, meaning women need to work harder and spend more than their male counterparts in order to achieve the same results.[113] Many studies cite fundraising and access to campaign financing as two of the greatest barriers to women in politics. As discussed previously, Canada has some of the most progressive legislation on political party financing, but could use greater enforcement and closure of some loopholes.

Money remains a barrier to women and other excluded groups in our political process. Limiting the duration of both nomination and election campaigns would certainly help to open up the process. Several political parties have special funds dedicated to assisting female candidates—such as the Judy LaMarsh Fund in the Liberal Party. These types of funds should be encouraged. Another solution that has been proposed to minimize the impact of big money in politics has been to restore the per-vote subsidy to political parties. This kind of public financing—which is used in many democracies—tends to level the playing field for those candidates and parties that do not have access to big-money networks—often women. In fact, the amount of the per-vote subsidy could be increased for female candidates in order to provide further incentives to political parties to nominate women in winnable ridings.

Many countries, such as France and Ireland, have implemented financial incentives or penalties to political parties in order to get more women nominated, which has tended to be successful in the long term. Mid-level party officials would be less likely to act as gatekeepers if they knew they would have to explain to the leadership why the party lost a significant chunk of money due to their inaction in promoting (or in some cases actions in discouraging) women candidates. Unlike quotas, incentives and disincentives would give parties flexibility while still institutionalizing the need for change.

---

113. Lisa Young, "Campaign Finance and Women's Representation in Canada and the United States," *The Delicate Balance between Political Equality and Freedom of Expression – Political Party and Campaign Finance in Canada and the United States*, (Stockholm: IDEA & Organization of American States, 2005): 48, 53–54; G.L. Sidhu and R. Meena, *Electoral Financing to Advance Women's Political Participation: A Guide for UNDP Support* (January 1, 2007), retrieved October 15, 2013, from http://iknowpolitics.org/sites/default/files/electoral_financing-en-ebook.pdf.

Mentors and Role Models

It has been proven that in countries where there are strong female role models in politics the number of women running increases. The appointment in Canada of a gender-equal cabinet in 2015 has been a leap forward in this regard. When society sees successful women in the highest leadership roles, it shifts our concepts of power and leadership from largely masculine traits to more feminine ones. This development has the added benefit of opening the door to men who display more feminine leadership styles (empathy, compassion, cooperation). The profiles of "winnability" and "star candidates" also begin to shift to include those traits. When young women and girls see themselves reflected in their leaders, it inspires them to think about politics and can do wonders to eliminate the "ambition gap" in politics.

Organizations like Equal Voice—a multi-partisan non-profit organization dedicated to increasing women's political participation in Canada—have several projects that help with mentorship and role modelling. One such project, Daughters of the Vote, will bring 338 young women to Ottawa this year to sit in Parliament to show what it could look like. Other projects, such as encouraging parents to take their daughters with them when they vote and a "Be her or support her" campaign, have had an impact and should be encouraged. Political parties have also established campaigns through social media to urge women to run for office, such as the Liberal Party's 2015 "Invite a woman to run" campaign. Such programs are successful because women often wait to be asked before considering running.

Mentorship between experienced women and those new to politics is also extremely useful. The biweekly candidate calls that I participated in as a candidate, and that I now lead as an MP, are often a lifeline to women who are running. After losing an election it can be very isolating for former candidates who plan to try a second time. On many occasions, it was knowing that other women were going through the same thing and solutions that they provided that kept me from giving up. I saw the same kind of powerful peer support when I managed iKNOW Politics, where women supported one another from the other side of the world. In one e-discussion I saw an indigenous Bolivian woman who had become mayor of her town, writing in Spanish, provide advice to a French-speaking woman in Mali who was running for her municipal council. In June 2016, women MPs from all parties came together to host an aboriginal blanket reconciliation ceremony on Parliament Hill as the launch of an all-party women's caucus. It is this kind of support that can create the "critical mass" that allows women to break down barriers.

Reforming the House of Commons

Recently I was talking to a group of fourteen-year-old girls who were visiting Parliament for the first time, and I asked them if they would run one day. The response was an emphatic "No!" I asked them why and the answer was that they had just come from Question Period and could not imagine working in that kind of environment. Most MPs will tell you that they are embarrassed when school groups or other visitors come to watch the daily round of heckling and booing and raucous applause that is Question Period. And yet it continues. For many Canadians, this is what Parliament looks like and it is keeping many good women and men from considering politics. The Speaker should be encouraged to use the tools at his or her disposal—such as naming a member—to establish better decorum in the House.

With two-thirds of the MPs elected in the 2015 election being new to Parliament, we have a unique opportunity to change the tone and culture of the House of Commons to one where there is more civility and cooperation. There are very few opportunities for cross-party cooperation in our Parliament. The entire structure is set up to be adversarial—even the spatial separation of political parties in the Chamber and in committees. I often wonder what would happen if we decided to mix up the seats in committee so that the government and opposition were not sitting across from one another. When I chaired the Special Committee on Pay Equity I made a deliberate attempt to never refer to committee members by their party affiliation but rather by their individual names. There are other changes that could be made to committees and to rules of procedure to ensure that Parliament works in a less adversarial way. I recently learned that a member of the opposition was in the same class as I was in university—after we had sat just metres from one another for months without ever having had a conversation. If there were more platforms for cross-party cooperation, the tone of the attacks during adversarial times would diminish as well, and more women would be encouraged to run.

Modernizing the parliamentary schedule to allow MPs to spend their time more efficiently would have a large impact on women and on men with young families. Having votes after Question Period rather than late into the evening, providing the sitting schedule in advance, ensuring that parliamentary break weeks correspond with most school holidays and eliminating Friday sittings would result in more women choosing to run. Currently on Fridays there are no committees, no major votes, and the House only sits for four-and-a-half hours. If those hours were redistributed over the course of the week, MPs from far-away ridings that have young families could return home on Thursday evening instead of Friday afternoon. This schedule would also allow MPs to have a full business day in their ridings every week, to meet with constituents and hear their concerns.

With modern technology there is no reason that MPs must be in Ottawa in order to do their parliamentary business. Society has changed over the past 150 years, but Parliament has not. Gone are the old days, when older men would take the train to Ottawa and deliberate among themselves over what was best for the country. Today, there is a greater expectation that MPs are accessible and listening to public input, and yet the balance of time spent in Ottawa compared to the constituency has not changed significantly. Eliminating Friday sittings has been the one consistent reform that women in Parliament have been discussing for decades. It has been done at the provincial level, and it would be the most obvious and easiest way to accommodate more women in Parliament.

Nominations

The party selection process is the one area that is most in need of reform. Political parties in Canada guard their independence with good reason. This is one aspect of our democratic process that has never come under much scrutiny. There is serious need for reform of the nominations process in order to elect more women. The rules need to be made more clear, consistent and transparent and they need to be rigorously enforced. There have been suggestions that to truly ensure fairness, nomination contests should be managed by Elections Canada rather than by political parties themselves. If this were the case, parties would still need to be able to do a vetting of candidates to ensure candidates reflect the party's values and support the basic tenets of its platform.

Whether managed by the parties or by an independent body, nomination contests should have time limits. For example, from the time the first contestant has filed papers and is given the go-ahead by the party to run, there should be a maximum amount of time until the contest is held—for instance, three months. This will ensure a level playing field, minimize the amount of time a candidate needs to take leave from work, and help to make the process more predictable and free from interference. The rules of procedure, application processes and timelines should be clearly available online, and rules should be strictly enforced. Candidate search committees should always include women, and local riding associations should not be given approval to hold a nomination meeting until they can show that they have made efforts to recruit women.

Party leaders should not have the right to appoint candidates except in cases of electoral urgency. There have been some who would go so far as to suggest that party leaders should not have the final sign-off on who the party's candidates are. The question of who has the final say over designating—or vetoing—a party candidate is a difficult one. The current law states that parties must designate who has this authority. Taking this duty away from the leader could lead to party cliques and gatekeepers taking control of the process, which would be even worse for women. Allowing parties to vet candidates and then having Elections Canada manage the actual nomination contest may be the best solution.

Conclusion

It has been one hundred years since some women in Canada first got the right to vote. We do not want to wait another one hundred years to achieve parity for women in the House of Commons. To achieve equal political participation of women in Parliament, major changes are needed: the role of party gatekeepers needs to be minimized through significant reforms and the opening up of party nomination processes; we need to change social biases and assumptions about women and about political leaders generally; Parliament needs to become a more inclusive and welcoming institution; and there need to be more platforms for cooperation between women and between parties.

While it is apparent that voluntary measures have not led to improvements in women's political representation, I do not think that implementing mandatory quotas for women in politics would work in Canada, given our strong political culture, which values local representation and independence of political parties. Giving political parties greater incentives (through financial penalties or rewards) to nominate more women would provide the motivation while still maintaining flexibility for parties in how to select candidates. I am in favour of greater public funding of political parties based on the number of votes, linked to the number of female candidates a party nominates.

While replacing the first-past-the-post electoral system would be a significant step in removing barriers to women, we need to be cautious that not all alternatives would necessarily be an improvement. The impact on women candidates, including intersectionality of gender with other identities, needs to be a major consideration when looking at any change to our electoral system. Regardless of which electoral system is chosen, it is imperative that party candidate selection processes be reformed to ensure that they are more open, transparent, predictable and independent from manipulation—and that rules are enforced.

Parliament itself needs to function in a more inclusive way—including eliminating Friday sittings, ensuring women are not limited to "soft" portfolios and women's issues, creating a more respectful tone in Question Period, reducing partisanship and party discipline, supporting the all-party women's caucus and providing more opportunities for cross-party cooperation. Finally, women need to form alliances with feminist men in order to achieve critical mass, and provide mentoring and peer support for one another. Civil society groups and media can help to change the negative way in which women political leaders are portrayed. Personal attacks and inflammatory rhetoric need to become socially unacceptable. As more women succeed in politics, a virtuous cycle will change our attitudes and we will become more inclusive about what is a strong political leader or a "star" candidate.

Equal political participation is a precondition for decision-making that is truly democratic. Different experiences and perspectives must have a voice at the table or they will not be represented in decisions. Often, making political processes more open to women has the effect of opening those processes to other excluded groups. Removing the barriers that prevent women from succeeding in electoral politics and shattering that glass ceiling paves the way for a whole generation of new political voices to be heard in Canada. I have seen women around the world risk their lives, their families and their personal security in order to take their place at the table. I have personally experienced what a difference it makes having women in the room. If we make the right changes today, then our daughters will stand beside our sons with equal voices in the House of Commons and in our country.

Social Media, Social Movements and Young-Voter Engagement

Niki Ashton

The trend was clear. Election after election, decade after decade, young voters were voting in smaller and smaller numbers in virtually every federal election. The decline in voter participation among young voters was even greater than the overall decline. Youth voter apathy was an international problem—faced across the board in developed democracies from the United States to the United Kingdom. The decline in turnout among youth in Canada received considerable attention and was seen as having a direct impact on overall voter turnout. A Statistics Canada report released the same month as the 2015 federal election stated that "It has been shown that the general decline in voter turnout is largely the result of a decrease in the voter turnout of youth." People were further struck by the fact that young people were engaged in social movements and political activity outside of elections, yet were not voting. Young people appeared to see little if any value in engaging in traditional politics. There was even speculation that millennials were going to be less engaged in the political process as they grew older, leading to a permanent shift downwards in voter participation.

Then came the 2015 federal election, with its dramatic increase in overall turnout, powered by an equally dramatic increase in the number of young voters. In my riding of Churchill–Keewatinook Aski in northern Manitoba, demographically one of the youngest ridings in the country, there was a spectacular increase in voter turnout of 16 percentage points. The numbers told only part of the story. Anyone involved in the election could not fail to notice the high degree to which young voters were engaged not only in voting but in political activity, particularly on social media. The diverse nature of the political activity on social media was also striking, from memes to selfies to videos to in-depth dialogue across multiple platforms. This shocking shift in voter participation in 2015 raises many questions about the causes and further implications. Why did this dramatic rise in young-voter turnout take place? Was this a unique event or does it represent a new trend of engagement of young people in politics? What role have social movements and social media played in the relationship between young people and electoral politics?

The Cutting-Edge Politics of Churchill–Keewatinook Aski

Churchill is a unique area of the country in many ways. The constituency is the same physical size as Sweden and has many isolated communities, twenty-one of which lack all-weather road access. As mentioned above, it is one of the youngest regions in the country. Not surprisingly social media, particularly Facebook, have become a major tool and influence: people use social media sites to communicate within their community, and with family and friends outside the community. Many also use them as a news source. With the exception of a few more-urban communities, there are few if any traditional media outlets that reach northern Manitoba households. Most communities do not have local newspapers. Thus, articles and media content shared on Facebook play an increasingly significant role in disseminating information. So do direct observations posted by people on the Internet. There are many times when people have posted information and it spreads throughout social media before being picked up by the mainstream media.

An interesting phenomenon can also occur when broadcast media footage receives widespread attention via northerners sharing the content on Facebook. In one case I asked a question in the House of Commons about a tragic fire in an aboriginal community in Saskatchewan. Footage of my question was shared extensively and viewed by several hundred thousand people. Another type of content crossover that is popular in Churchill–Keewatinook Aski is watching clips from the Aboriginal Peoples Television Network (APTN) through social media. Original YouTube content is also widely viewed, with one example being a video I worked on with young residents to fight against job cuts by a mining company in my hometown of Thompson. It was picked up and shared by popular US political commentator Michael Moore and was watched by more than 27,000 people. In addition, YouTube videos of my questions during Question Period and debate in the House of Commons often receive widespread viewership among my constituents, particularly when they originate with a media outlet.

One of the appeals of social media in my constituency is the opportunity for two-way communication. Young people in particular use social media as a way to directly communicate with elected representatives. On my end, it is often time-consuming to respond to questions and concerns, but it is absolutely critical. Another aspect of social media and politics that is often overlooked is that not all social media communication is political. I consider it necessary to ensure there are many personal elements in communication through social media.

One of the biggest mistakes that people in politics make is assuming everyone is into politics as much as they are. Many people, particularly young people, are also interested in the human side of politicians. People often go to Facebook to get some personal sense of a candidate or elected official, which is one of the reasons I draft all my own social media content. Quite frankly, people can see through posts on Facebook or Twitter that are not authentically and directly written by the person they represent. Articles and analyses tend to focus on social media's role in elections, but the experience in northern Manitoba demonstrates the importance of maintaining ongoing social media communication with young people.

The Myth of Youth Apathy

Any suggestion that youth are apathetic is a myth. Despite the previously low election turnouts on a national scale, there has been evidence that young people are more involved in general civic engagement and campaigning than older generations are. A study conducted by Samara Canada for the Canadian Alliance of Student Associations (CASA) showed that when we look at rates of participation in political and civic life *beyond* voting, young Canadians rate 11 percent higher, on average, than older Canadians across eighteen different forms of political participation. The study showed young voters were more involved in activities including discussing politics and political issues face to face or over the phone, working with others in their communities, volunteering for a candidate or campaign, and protesting or demonstrating (34 percent for under age thirty, versus 15 percent of those aged fifty-six and over).

The 2015 Canadian federal election saw a 12-percent increase in participation among the youngest potential voters. Another study commissioned by CASA included a survey of one thousand Canadians aged eighteen to twenty-five that confirmed that young Canadians had voted in greater numbers than in the past. The study showed that contact from parties, candidates and elected officials is influential. Among young Canadians who reported experiencing this contact, 61 percent agreed that they are "affected by the decisions made by elected officials" every day. Of the young Canadians who reported no contact, only 22 percent agreed. Almost half of Canadians under thirty had never been contacted by any federal parties, MPs or candidates, compared to only one quarter of Canadians aged fifty-six and older. To consider the broader context of why people vote, Samara Canada has identified six reasons why people vote:

- Duty
- Social pressure
- Something's at stake
- Habit (after their third time voting, people are more likely to continue doing so)
- No barriers (around ID/eligibility, knowledge of when and where to vote, physical accessibility of the polls)
- Contact (people are more likely to vote once they've been asked to)

Compared to prior elections, many of these factors were accentuated in 2015, particularly the "what is at stake" factor. Evidently, young people saw the election as important and encouraged others to vote. David McGrane, a political science professor at the University of Saskatchewan, has conducted research showing the electoral impact of younger people voting: "High voter turnout of young people can actually change Canadian politics, it can change how the campaigns are run, the ideas that come up during the campaign, and have drastic effects in terms of which parties succeed and which parties fail."

Young People in Parties and Office

In recent years, political parties have stressed the involvement of young people. The Liberal Party and New Democratic Party have added provisions to their constitutions establishing youth wings. An even more fundamental element of young people being involved in the political process is actually running for and being elected to Parliament. I first ran when I was twenty-two years old and was elected when I was twenty-six years old, at the time the youngest woman in the House of Commons. The 2011 federal election broke all the records in terms of electing young people. In many ways, the significant number of youth elected in 2011 was a precursor of the youth engagement in 2015. But another key element is the degree to which mainstream parties and leaders focus on issues of concern to young people. In the 2016 Democratic nomination contest in the US, 74-year-old Bernie Sanders captured the imagination and received the support of young voters.

Social Media

Canada is an online country and young people are more online than any other age group. At 84 percent, Canada is tied for third with Great Britain in terms of global Internet penetration, and Canadians aged eighteen to thirty-four (48 percent) are more likely than their middle-aged (35 percent) and older (22 percent) counterparts to be "active" on social media. The Internet engagement of young people is borne out in 2015 Canadian Social Media Usage Statistics for specific social media: 16 percent of survey respondents overall used Instagram, with the youngest Canadians at 32 percent; 25 percent of survey respondents overall used Twitter, while 32 percent of young Canadians used it; 59 percent of survey respondents used Facebook, with 75 percent of Canadian youth using it.

There is also a connection between Internet use and politics. A 2013 Ipsos Public Affairs study that examined the use of social media for discourse and information on public policy, social and political issues showed that more than half (52 percent) of Canadians were using social media "actively" (29 percent) to make their voices heard or at least "passively" (23 percent) to gain a greater understanding of the issues. Interestingly, those most likely to be actively engaged were earning lower incomes (45 percent), while those earning higher incomes (29 percent) were least likely to be active. Half (50 percent) of Canadians with higher levels of education engaged in social media actively.

The connection between social media and political involvement is more than coincidental. Ryerson University professor Daniel Rubenson, who specializes in voting behaviour, has stressed just how connected young people are. "This newest generation of voters is probably the best equipped to deal with that kind of information overload," he said. "[They are] the first generation that has grown up having the internet their entire lives and being very media and social media savvy." International findings are similar. One study covering samples in Australia, the US and the UK suggested a strong, positive relationship between social media use and political engagement among young people. Brad Lavigne, key strategist in Jack Layton's 2011 breakthrough election for the NDP, has identified that social media can help in volunteer/supporter recruitment, engagement between elections and mobilization, through calls of action to donate money, volunteer one's time, recruit friends and family, and of course get out and vote.

It is important, however, to recognize that young people's use of and connection to social media and politics is complex. Millennials' political opinions are influenced by online interactions as well as interactions that do not involve the Internet. What is clear is that Canada in general is connected to the Internet and young people in particular are well connected. Social media is a key factor in how young people connect with each other, with their communities and with politics—and it has also been instrumental in driving social movements, not only by facilitating information and discussion, but also by organizing direct political action such as protests.

Social Movements

Elections and political party activity are not the only dimensions of political activity. Social movements attract people around political action on key issues. Even before the 2015 election, it was widely accepted that millennials were active in social movements. Social movements have been part of the political equation for many years, but what has been striking recently is how more and more movements are forming in short periods of time on many different issues—particularly in Canada. Young people are not only involved in these social movements but in many cases are leading them right from the beginning:

- Movements related to the impact of globalization (including Occupy) have focused on the detrimental effects of bad trade deals on jobs and living standards in Canada and throughout the world. The environmental movement has concentrated on issues ranging from global climate change to more local initiatives such as, in my constituency, opposing the shipping of crude oil along the Hudson Bay rail line.The LGBTQ community and its allies have been active on issues ranging from same-sex marriage to homophobia, and have focused on specific events such as pride parades, which have spread even to small communities such as Steinbach, Manitoba. One of the largest indigenous mass movements in Canadian history, Idle No More sparked hundreds of teach-ins, rallies and protests, beginning as a series of teach-ins throughout Saskatchewan to protest federal bills that eroded indigenous sovereignty and environmental protections.

- Indigenous women and advocacy organizations have mobilized to demand action on the epidemic of missing and murdered indigenous women: 1,017 women and girls identified as indigenous were murdered between 1980 and 2012—a homicide rate roughly four-and-a-half times higher than that for all other women in Canada.

- The 2012 Quebec student protests were a series of demonstrations led by student unions against Liberal premier Jean Charest's plan to raise university tuition, including a student strike and a rally of upwards of 500,000 protesters in Montreal.

- Black Lives Matter started in the United States and is spreading across Canada on the premise that Canadian police, media and society exhibit anti-black racism.

The Future

Is the dramatic increase in turnout, particularly among young voters in 2015, a new reality? Or will it become a historic anomaly similar to the increase in the US of young-voter turnout during the first election of Barack Obama, followed by lower voter participation rates in 2012? A similar question can be asked about young people, social media and politics. Much of what has been written about the impact of social media in election campaigns has focused on Obama's original presidential campaign in 2008. But by 2016 Bernie Sanders in the US and Jeremy Corbyn in the UK had also thrived on social media and connected to social movements to build powerful political forces. The ability to organize live events, fundraise and have people connect via social media are proving to be especially impressive. Significant evidence continues to build that young people will vote if they have communication from parties or candidates, political engagement with their peers and a broader sense through social media that voting can make a difference.

Whatever the patterns of voter participation have been over the past twenty years, the updated reality is that while young people are participating in social movements and civic life in many different fashions, they have also proven to be fully capable of voting in federal elections. It turns out that young Canadians are less cynical about politics and the electoral process than previously assumed—and they showed up at the polls in significant numbers in 2015. One of the assumptions behind the previous low turnouts was that young people felt their votes did not matter. But even in the 2011 election, which had a lower turnout, young people's votes made a difference in the NDP's breakthrough to official Opposition. And the 2015 election showed young people their votes had made a difference by voting out the Harper government and voting in the Trudeau government.

In fact every related study, survey and poll indicates that there is major potential for tremendous growth in engagement of young Canadians in both the immediate sense and in upcoming years. The previous cohort analysis that assumed millennials would bring down voter turnout over time may no longer apply. If the 2015 election has kicked off a new trend, millennial participation may actually increase voter participation to a level that has not been seen in twenty years. A factor in this potential direction will be whether political parties can sustain the involvement of young people. A report by the Broadbent

Institute found that 70 percent of young Canadians feel their views are ignored by politicians. The federal government that was elected in 2015 may merely validate this feeling of alienation, but alternatively if the many young people who participated in the 2015 federal election see their aspirations reflected in government policies and programs, they will be more likely to vote in the future.

Every analysis of voter participation, of any age group, indicates that the most likely voters are people who have voted in the past. Voting and participating in the democratic process is habit-forming. As journalist Susan Delacourt remarked after the 2015 election, "Of course, it's always possible that this surge of young voters will fade away as surely as all the excitement over the new government. But we do know that voting is a bit of a habit; young voters turn into older voters, and maybe now that these eighteen-to-twenty-five-year-olds have had a taste of democracy, they'll stick with it as they move into middle age."

But when it comes to young people in Canada, as of 2015 there can be no doubt. Not only are they not apathetic, they are active and connected. And they have created a new activism that connects social media with social movements. Young people have made it clear that they are not just the future in terms of politics, they are very much the here and now as well. They have made a real commitment to politics in the broadest sense, including voting. The real question is whether politicians and political institutions can live up to the aspirations of young Canadians today and into the future.

Sources

Canadian Labour Congress. "Young Voters: Ignored, Not Apathetic," September 23, 2015. http://canadianlabour.ca/news/news-archive/young-voters-ignored-not-apathetic.

Coletto, David. "The Next Canada: Politics, Political Engagement, and Priorities of Canada's Next Electoral Powerhouse: Young Canadians," April 19, 2016. http://abacusdata.ca/the-next-canada-politics-political-engagement-and-priorities-of-canadas-next-electoral-powerhouse-young-canadians/.

Delacourt, Susan. "Youth a New 'Electoral Powerhouse' in Canada," April 20, 2016. http://thetyee.ca/Opinion/2016/04/20/Youth-Electoral-Powerhouse/.

Dorfmann, Jessica. "The Power of Young Voters: Canada's Historic Election," November 4, 2015. http://hir.harvard.edu/power-young-voters-canadas-historic-election/.

Hilderman, Jane. "Tackling the Myth of Politically Apathetic Young Canadians," October 15, 2016. http://www.huffingtonpost.ca/jane-hilderman/youth-vote_b_8272398.html.

Ipsos. "More Than Half (52%) of Canadians Are 'Engaged' with Politics, Public Policy, and Social Issues Online," June 19, 2013. http://www.ipsos-na.com/news-polls/pressrelease.aspx?id=6156.

Kelsh, Chaz. "How Social Media Influences Millennials' Political Views," December 3, 2015. http://journalistsresource.org/studies/society/social-media/facebook-millennial-politics-election.

King, Robin Levinson. "Youth Voters Made Big Gains in Oct. Election: Statistics Canada," February 22, 2016. https://www.thestar.com/news/canada/2016/02/22/youth-voters-made-big-gains-in-oct-election-statistics-canada.html.

Lavigne, Brad. "The Whole New Ballgame of Social Media," January 5, 2015. http://hkstrategies.ca/old-news/the-whole-new-ballgame-of-social-media/.

Mathurin, Yasmine. "Social Media Helps First-Time Voters Get Involved in Politics," October 22, 2015. http://ryersonian.ca/social-media-helps-first-time-voters-get-involved-in-politics/.

McKinnon, Melody. "2015 Canadian Social Media Usage Statistics," January 12, 2015. http://canadiansinternet.com/2015-canadian-social-media-usage-statistics/.

McWhinney, Andrew. "Politicians Would Do Good by Genuinely Appealing to Youth," January 26, 2016. https://thegatewayonline.ca/2016/01/politicians-would-do-good-by-genuinely-appealing-to-youth/.

Turcotte, Martin. "Political Participation and Civic Engagement of Youth," October 7, 2015. http://www.statcan.gc.ca/pub/75-006-x/2015001/article/14232-eng.htm.

Wikipedia, "2012 Quebec student protests," February 12, 2017. https://en.m.wikipedia.org/wiki/2012_Quebec_student_protests.

Wihbey, John. "How Does Social Media Use Influence Political Participation and Civic Engagement? A Meta-Analysis," October 18,

2015. http://journalistsresource.org/studies/politics/digital-democracy/social-media-influence-politics-participation-engagement-meta-analysis.

Xenos, Michael, Ariadne Vromen and Brian D. Loader. "The Great Equalizer? Patterns of Social Media Use and Youth Political Engagement in Three Advanced Democracies," January 3, 2014. http://www.tandfonline.com/doi/abs/10.1080/1369118X.2013.871318.

Introducing the Assembly of the Federation: The House of Sober *First* Thought

Scott Simms

I t started out as a normal meeting of the Standing Committee on Canadian Heritage, but that day a great debate was sparked, with potential for miraculous things to follow. In the context of how we could structure a celebration of Canada's 150th birthday in 2017, a government MP asked to what extent our children truly understood Canadian history. Several excellent points came from MPs of all parties representing all corners of our country. We spoke of the genesis of a national program to teach young Canadians the great accomplishments of a large nation with a relatively small population. Classes in British Columbia, Nova Scotia and Nunavut would discover how thousands of people fleeing nations around the world set sail for Pier 21 in Halifax to escape tyranny and poverty. They came here with little to nothing in personal wealth and helped build our nation into a world economic leader in less than 150 years. We envisioned a national education program to augment existing history courses throughout Canada, supported by the latest digital technology and coordinated by a federal agency.

In my twelve years in the House of Commons, this particular meeting stands out because of the excitement it inspired in everyone there. As a parliamentarian you do not often take part in a discussion that stirs something in your soul and makes you realize why you decided to put your name on the ballot. But as the debate began to coalesce in a rare political consensus, something typically Canadian happened. One MP blurted out a phrase that always grinds debate to a screeching halt: "But that is provincial jurisdiction." With that, a wet, heavy blanket was thrown over a lovely campfire discussion.

As disappointing as the outcome was, the provincial jurisdiction argument is a valid one outlined in sections 91 and 92 of our Constitution. Without a doubt, most national political struggles in our history can be attributed to this ongoing power struggle between prime minister and premier, minister and minister, and our federal public service in endless battle with provincial bureaucrats. Sometimes it is hard to believe that this country has achieved such a level of cohesion when such large and impermeable walls exist between provinces and around our government in Ottawa.

I realize my characterization of provincial–federal relations is harsh, but if there could be a greater understanding between our provincial and federal politicians, so much more could be achieved. Technology provides us with a wonderful opportunity to engage in meaningful dialogue from coast to coast to coast; we can no longer use the excuse that there is too much space between us. The fault does not lie with our inability to digitally connect, it lies with our political dialogue. To break away from the tired, old excuses from narrow-minded politicians and bureaucrats, I am proposing a bold, new institution that structures a dialogue among the average, hard-working members of our provincial assemblies—those more commonly known as backbenchers.

Council of the Federation

Today, the most prominent platform for interprovincial discussion among our provincial politicians is the Council of the Federation. Discussions between our premiers used to take place only when required for a particular matter such as health transfers or constitutional reform. But on December 5, 2003, the Council of the Federation was announced in Charlottetown, PEI, following an earlier suggestion of the concept by Quebec premier Jean Charest. Since then, the first ministers have met twice per year with the chair rotating among the provinces and territories. The council's primary focus is to "work collaboratively to strengthen the Canadian federation by fostering a constructive relationship among the provinces and territories, and with the federal government."[114]

I commend the achievements of the council, such as the establishment of funding arrangements and an initial agreement for interprovincial trade. The larger provinces, including Ontario and Quebec, have worked on arrangements to reduce emissions and address climate change by using a similar system. My proposal sets out to augment the council and other interprovincial meetings by offering a forum for politicians who currently have no opportunity to engage in the national discussion. We know them as backbenchers—they exist in all of our legislatures and fulfill a vital function of our parliamentary system. But currently, the chance to discuss national issues in a national forum is limited for them. We are missing out on an opportunity to strengthen our federation with the experiences and ideas that these elected officials from across the country can bring to the table.

MLAS, MPPS, MNAS and MHAS deal with the most vital areas of government day after day while assisting constituents, lobbying our bureaucracy, attending endless meetings, taking on committee responsibilities, and making numerous public appearances. But how can they make a more national contribution? How can we structure and facilitate a dialogue among a group of this size, with such a wide variety of experiences and perspectives? In October 2005 I had the experience of a lifetime when I visited a political forum that inspired me to write this piece: the parliamentary assembly of the Council of Europe.

The Council of Europe

The concept of a united Europe and the establishment of pan-European institutions to freely and peacefully exchange ideas and policies had its roots in the nineteenth century. However, nothing truly took shape until the mid-twentieth century. The dominant force today is the European Union, whose twenty-eight (soon to be twenty-seven) nations draft, study, debate and enact legislation. Its legislators are known as "Members of the European Parliament" or MEPS. But before there was a European Union or even the European Common Market, there was an institution called the Council of Europe.

---

114. "About Canada's Premiers, "http://canadaspremiers.ca/en/about.

On September 19, 1946, British prime minister Sir Winston Churchill called for the creation of "the United States of Europe." Shortly after, many leading European politicians and academics met on several occasions to create an entity to improve European relations. Savaged by two world wars, Europe had become desperate to find a way to avoid conflict. On May 5, 1949, the Council of Europe was created by the Treaty of London, fulfilling a dream sought by not only Churchill but also millions of Europeans who no longer wanted to engage in narrow-minded, nationalist rhetoric and jingoism. Citizens were demanding new leadership to recognize basic human rights and began pressuring politicians from all ideologies to achieve a greater understanding—peacefully.

Today, the Council of Europe flourishes and is focused on human rights, democracy and the rule of law. There are two main institutions that make up the council. First there is the committee of ministers, made up of foreign ministers from the forty-seven member states. The second institution, and the one that I intend to focus on in this chapter, is the parliamentary assembly. The parliamentary assembly of the Council of Europe is located in Strasbourg, France, consisting of 324 parliamentarians from a wide array of political parties, movements and ideologies. They meet four times each year for full-week sessions, in January, April, June and October. Parliamentarians are not directly elected to this assembly; they are backbenchers chosen by their national parties to represent their views in Strasbourg. British members of Parliament sit next to national assembly members from France, members from the Italian Chamber of Deputies, Swedish Riksdag and German Bundestag.

At first blush, one might assume members arrive in Strasbourg with an intent to foist their domestic priorities upon the entire continent of Europe. I have attended many of these sessions and saw this dynamic take place on many occasions, including visceral and self-serving debates between Ukraine and Russia, and Russia and Georgia. I witnessed numerous insults being hurled between Turkey and Greece and a barrage of guttural pronouncements by members representing right-wing parties. However, I still found myself continually astonished by the well-spoken, mature and greatly informative level of debate from all forty-seven nations.

Despite the substantial amount of work that is accomplished, the Council of Europe faces a great deal of skepticism in part because it cannot make binding laws. But it does have the power to promote international agreements, which is why the most famous section of the Council of Europe is the European Court of Human Rights, which enforces the European Convention on Human Rights. The parliamentary assembly actually appoints the judges of the European Court of Human Rights, as well as questioning heads of state invited to the assembly, assigning members to observe elections in member states, and monitoring laws and constitutions of its member states for any legal requests. And mostly, members spend their time drafting, debating and amending motions and resolutions that, if accepted, go back to their home states to be considered as guidelines for new domestic laws.

For example, Resolution 2123, titled Culture and Democracy, was passed by the assembly in June 2016, urging "stronger recognition of the role that culture can play in upholding democratic principles and values, and building inclusive societies...Democratic institutions and democratic laws will not effectively work unless they build on a democratic culture." Vigorous debate rallied around the importance of supporting the arts and the artists who spend their lives expressing who we are as different societies. In the end, the resolution overwhelmingly urged member states of Europe to invest in cultural activity and education equally with investments in the economy, infrastructure, security and all other areas seen as crucial to Europe's stability.

I can recall another example from my first experience with the Council of Europe. In 2005, the assembly chose to draft and debate a resolution calling on its member states and the European Union to ban all seal products from Canada because of cruel and inhumane hunting practices. Since I was a member of Parliament from Newfoundland and Labrador, which has one of the largest populations of seal hunters, I was attending the council to defend the seal harvest. As observers, we were given the opportunity to intervene but could not vote. In the end, the assembly chose to accept the resolution, and today a ban on seal products from Canada extends through all twenty-eight nations of the European Union.

No member state of the Council of Europe is compelled to immediately draft legislation in response to a parliamentary assembly motion, or even to do so at all. But evidence does show that a large collection of laws, rules and conventions have been adopted by all forty-seven nations in support of the work of the Council of Europe in Strasbourg.

Although I still don't agree with the seal ban, this European model has inspired me to promote a forum for provincial politicians to lead a national discussion that would strengthen our federation. But this is not a new concept for Canada. It has been proposed before and was in fact the original concept for our Council of the Federation.

The Original Council of the Federation

In 1976, the country was in political shock as it awoke to the election of a Parti Québécois government in Quebec City. The fight suddenly *got real* when a party was elected on a platform of separating from the rest of the country. Compared to the relative peace I have witnessed over the past ten years in Ottawa, I cannot imagine the panic that ensued. Separatist sentiment was running at an all-time high for francophones in Quebec, while push-back emerged in the form of anti-Quebec feelings in other provinces. Less than a decade after our centennial celebrations in 1967 and the World's Fair held in Montreal that same year, the realities of maintaining a love of being Canadian—and maintaining a federal constitution—were being tested at the highest stakes.

In 1977, the Pierre Trudeau government created a task force on Canadian unity called the Pepin–Robarts Commission, led by former cabinet minister Jean-Luc Pepin and former premier of Ontario John Robarts. Six prominent Canadians were chosen to round out the commission, and it embarked on a tour of the country asking for public submissions. Upon completion, it was required to supply the government with a report and specific recommendations. By all accounts, the meetings were quite stormy as Canadians let loose with their frustrations and suggestions. When complete, the staggering amount of input gathered took some time to digest, organize, translate and disseminate.

The Pepin–Robarts Commission ended up proposing a "restructured federalism" in order to accommodate the duality of our cultures and address our vast regionalism. What was most striking to many—and likely disconcerting for the inner circles of power in Ottawa—was the call for the national and provincial levels of government to act as equals in a true federal partnership. Today, these suggestions for devolution of power to the provinces may seem rather perfunctory and normal, especially after the great constitutional debates of the 1980s and 1990s. However, in 1977 these recommendations boldly charted new territory in federal–provincial relations.

In some of its most striking recommendations, the commission called for a revamped Supreme Court and a new charter of rights to be entrenched in the Constitution, and the electoral system to include a form of proportional representation. But another proposal pertained to Parliament as well as major reform in the Senate—a change that would require buy-in from all provinces as required by the Constitution. The commission called for the Senate to be reconstituted as "the Council of the Federation," where provincial governments would send delegations to debate federal legislation.

This highly contentious proposal was not clear on why the Senate should be abolished, but it did advance the Council of the Federation as the "house of sober second thought" on matters of provincial jurisdiction, certain treaties, and issues arising from first ministers' meetings. However, matters of exclusive federal jurisdiction would not have needed the approval of this new council, so the abolition of the Senate would have left no secondary study of new federal laws. I suspect the commission was responding to negative public feedback regarding political patronage in the Senate, but I fail to understand why it could not still operate in *parallel* to a Council of the Federation, using the Senate chamber at different times.

The composition of the Pepin–Robarts version of the Council of the Federation would also undoubtedly raise concerns among provincial governments. The commission recommended having sixty voting members to be allocated by provincial populations. Smaller provinces, however, would likely prefer a distribution similar to the Senate's, in which all regions are represented equally at twenty-four seats each. In my opinion, anything that serves as a "house of sober second thought" in a country as large as Canada must be composed of equal regional representation. (I may be accused of a personal bias, since the province I represent is certainly one of the smallest.)

Another weakness of the Pepin–Robarts model requires that the delegates of provincial governments act under instruction and be headed by a delegate of cabinet rank. If we are sending delegates to Ottawa to act as federal policy analysts under the watchful eyes of their provincial executives, why send them at all? Any angst or trepidation felt by any premier can be aired through meetings of the first ministers, which are now held on a regular basis. In addition, ministers of health, education, natural resources, etc., meet regularly throughout the year to discuss policy concerns and federal legislation. So if the premiers and provincial cabinets were to also have tight control over their council delegations, these elaborate meetings composed of sixty delegates would be a redundant waste of time, energy and money.

The best of intentions by the commission must be applauded, as the concept of provincial politicians debating national issues is an ideal forum for better national cohesion. But the Council of the Federation proposed in the Pepin–Roberts Commission report is fraught with weaknesses in achieving a stronger federation. Its road map would likely grind us to a halt and certainly would not offer an adequate replacement for our Senate. The Trudeau government had deeper concerns for the decentralist theme of the entire Pepin–Roberts report and wisely decided to drop it. Although much different than originally proposed, a Council of the Federation did eventually appear under different circumstances in 2003.

The Assembly of the Federation

As flawed as the original concept was in 1977, the idea of provincial politicians from across Canada coming together to propose, draft, debate, amend and vote on issues is a positive vision that we cannot afford to let go. So we should do it right. Earlier, I outlined my experiences with the Council of Europe and in particular the parliamentary assembly that brings together elected officials from forty-seven nations. This assembly has a storied history of promoting best practices of governing in all areas of public discourse, most notably in human rights. It is time for Canada to take the next logical step to strengthen our federation by remodelling our Council of the Federation after an assembly composed of regional politicians who are not members of cabinet. It is time for us to embrace and welcome the knowledge and experiences of our backbench provincial politicians from all regions and parties to convene as Canada's Assembly of the Federation.

Although it would require the use of the Senate chamber, in no way do I envision the assembly as a replacement for the Senate. What I am proposing will provide a house of sober *first* thought for the House of Commons, while the Senate can continue to scrutinize federal legislation and continue its committee work. There are three general criteria when choosing which provincial politicians would share the seats of the Senate chamber:

1. They must not be members of the executive council in their home province.

Currently, the Council of the Federation along with myriad cross-Canada ministerial meetings provide a venue for our provincial executive councils to exchange ideas and dialogue over matters vital to the federation. Together, they bring forward concerns to our federal government regularly throughout the year. Allowing them to participate in the Assembly of the Federation would be redundant and in many cases overkill.

2. The number of seats per province would be based on the current formula within the Senate.

The original Senate was configured to provide equal representation from Canada's regions, consisting of twenty-four senators each from the West (British Columbia, Alberta, Saskatchewan and Manitoba); Ontario; Quebec; and the Maritimes (New Brunswick, PEI and Nova Scotia). Accommodations were later made to include Newfoundland with six seats after it joined Canada in 1949, and one from each of the territories, to bring the total to 105. The current makeup of the Senate goes a long way toward achieving an optimal balance between population and regional representation, though I am cognizant of angst regarding under-representation of provinces where population booms have created distortions in the formula. Also, having only one seat from each of the three territories would run counter to the purpose of reflecting diverse opinions from different parties, in this case the North. But for now, I will refer to the current distribution of seats in the Senate as the model.

3. Within the provincial delegations, the seats will be awarded to the members in proportion to the party standings of their respective home legislatures.

Let us now go across the country to see the face of the Assembly of the Federation, made up of provincial members from different parties based on how many seats they currently hold in their province. The calculation would need to be updated regularly, as provincial political dynamics can change with elections, by-elections, floor crossings and retirements. The chart below assigns seats to the provinces based on current rules of the Senate, and further assigns each of those seats to provincial parties based on the legislature standings at the beginning of the year. For the sake of this example, I calculated the seat allocations by provincial standings that are current to January 1, 2017:

British Columbia

3 BC Liberal, 3 NDP

Alberta

3 NDP, 2 Wildrose, 1 Progressive Conservative

Saskatchewan

5 Saskatchewan Party, 1 NDP

Manitoba

4 Progressive Conservative, 2 NDP

Ontario

13 Liberal, 7 Progressive Conservative, 4 NDP

Quebec

14 Liberal, 5 Parti Québécois, 4 Coalition Avenir Québec, 1 Québec solidaire

New Brunswick

6 Liberal, 4 Progressive Conservative

Prince Edward Island

3 Liberal, 1 Progressive Conservative

Nova Scotia

7 Liberal, 2 Progressive Conservative, 1 NDP

Newfoundland and Labrador

5 Liberal, 1 Progressive Conservative

According to the Senate layout, each of the three territories receives one seat. Nunavut and the Northwest Territories have territorial legislatures that do not utilize the party system, so the Speaker of their legislatures could choose a delegate for each calendar year. The Yukon does utilize the party system, so based on January 1, 2017, it would have one representative for the Liberal Party. All provinces would also need to provide alternatives for replacing the primary delegates when such a need arises.

The Assembly of the Federation in Action
And how would the Assembly of the Federation be assembled within the Senate chamber? An obvious seating plan would see colleagues from each province organized in provincial blocks. However, such an arrangement would not help further a truly national debate and would most certainly make it more difficult to come to a consensus. Instead, I propose that members sit with others of the same political affiliation and ideology. With ten provinces and three territories represented in a 105-seat legislature, the debates and the deliberations hopefully will coalesce around ideologies of right, left and centre. That is the way it should be in any modern democracy—and it should be no different in this forum, despite the unique regional concerns represented.

Party structures and caucuses must be set up to organize the debates and achieve consensus through caucus discussions, in addition to the debate on the floor. The Liberal Party of Canada has close organizational ties with the Ontario Liberal Party and the provincial Liberal parties in Atlantic Canada, so working together interprovincially would likely come naturally. Similarly, the New Democratic Party's national and provincial wings have long partnered very closely on virtually all policies and organizational machinery. The national Conservative Party specifically avoids initiating provincial counterparts of the same name, but there are several ideological Conservative entities by different names, notably the Saskatchewan Party, the Wildrose Party and the Coalition Avenir Québec (CAQ).

Because the members of the Assembly of the Federation would be backbenchers, no strict party discipline would need to apply. This is not at all a weakness of this concept; in fact, it could prove to be one of its greatest strengths. Not to be excessively Pollyannaish about how members from different provinces could easily jell for the sake of debate, conservatives of different provincial parties from west to east to north have far more in common than do card-carrying Liberals across the entire country. Therefore, "big tent" provincial parties that include supporters of multiple ideologies or federal parties—for example, the

BC Liberals—would not need to whip their members to vote together or even to serve in the same caucus; however, these members manage to bridge the divide within their provincial party, so it isn't a stretch to imagine them doing so in the same Assembly caucus as well. The outlier province regarding national caucus participation is Quebec. The composition outlined earlier provides five seats for the Parti Québécois and one seat for Québec solidaire. Despite their ultimate goal to secede from Canada, since the early 1970s the two parties have pushed substantial reforms and legislation on the left side of the political spectrum, and from that common ground could be great partners within this caucus arrangement.

The parliamentary assembly of Europe features several caucuses grouped together around common political ideologies. What makes this assembly so successful is that the MPs and senators are not organized by nation or region, but by political principles and beliefs: the European People's Party (EPP) is generally conservative, the Socialist Group (SOC) consists of left-leaning progressive parties, and the Alliance of Liberals and Democrats for Europe (ALDE) consists of centrist parties. When Canadian MPs have attended as observers, the Liberals have participated in the ALDE caucus, Conservatives in the EPP and the NDP in the SOC. By not using the names of registered national or provincial parties, groups can be formed with greater ease and less awkwardness.

So if the Assembly of the Federation existed in Canada today, what would the seating map look like? Using the political groups that I have suggested along with a few assumptions of my own, here is how the political groups might look in a current Canadian Assembly of the Federation:

Alliance of Liberals and Progressives: 52 seats

Quebec Liberal Party 13, Ontario Liberals 13, Nova Scotia Liberals 7, New Brunswick Liberals 6, Newfoundland and Labrador Liberals 5, BC Liberals 4, PEI Liberals 3, Yukon Liberals 1

Canadian Conservative Alliance: 31 seats

Ontario Progressive Conservatives 7, Saskatchewan Party 5, Manitoba Progressive Conservatives 4, Coalition Avenir Québec 4, New Brunswick Progressive Conservative Party 4, Alberta Wildrose Party 2, Nova Scotia Progressive Conservative Party 2, Alberta Progressive

Conservatives 1, PEI Progressive Conservatives 1, Newfoundland and Labrador PC Party 1

Social Democratic Alliance: 14 seats

Ontario NDP 4, BC NDP 3, Alberta NDP 3, Manitoba NDP 2, Saskatchewan NDP 1, Nova Scotia NDP 1)

I've left eight remaining seats not grouped with any particular ideology: five seats to the Parti Québécois, one seat to Québec solidaire and one seat each to the Northwest Territories and Nunavut, which don't have parties. These territorial members could choose a political group to join or sit on their own.

One observation that arises from speculating about how ideological caucuses might look based on current provincial seat counts is that no grouping would have the majority of the assembly. As I experienced in the House of Commons from 2004 to 2011, minority legislatures tend to provide interesting—and at times suspenseful—votes. As in any sport where combatants engage, a Speaker or chair is required to administer the rules and keep the peace. I propose that the Speaker's role be determined before the session to ensure adequate prerequisite work and familiarization with the role and institution upon arrival of the members. An easy rule of thumb could be to refer to the chairmanship of the Council of the Federation, where each year provincial premiers are designated chair and vice-chair of the council; the corresponding speakers of those same provinces could serve as Speaker and deputy speaker of the assembly.

How Do We Proceed?

Like the parliamentary assembly of the Council of Europe, the Canadian assembly would need to draft, introduce, debate, amend and vote on motions. Canadian parliamentarians have grown accustomed to Westminster parliamentary procedure, so we should stick to the same rule book. But since the assembly will meet only on a few occasions per year and will not legislate, the daily proceedings of the House of Commons should not be followed directly. Regrettably, I see little use for the spectacle of a highly theatrical and raucous Question Period. Since the assembly will be primarily concerned with motions put forward for debate and vote, the rules should be based on the standing orders of the House of Commons, illustrated and explained in *House of Commons Procedure and Practice*, edited by Audrey O'Brien and Marc Bosc.

But how do these motions for the assembly get started? I am tempted to suggest that this forum should adopt a no-holds-barred attitude toward what is to be discussed, like other assemblies and forums composed of different nations. However, we are still one nation functioning as a constitutional federation, so debating issues of federal jurisdiction would not serve much purpose. Despite this limitation, there should still be a wide scope regarding subject matter. A simple rule could be applied that all motions must relate to issues of complete or shared provincial jurisdiction. Examples of such issues include health, education and skills training of provincial jurisdiction, and topics of environment, economic development and fisheries under shared responsibilities between provincial and federal governments.

Another function of the assembly that must be initiated is permanent committees. I say *permanent* committees (or standing committees) because it would be inefficient to form committees based on a single motion. The obvious committees for this assembly would be health, education (which may include post-secondary education), science and technology, agriculture, fisheries, indigenous affairs and other areas where provincial and federal ministries coexist. Permanent committees could also address topics of a broader nature such as rural issues, urban issues, arts and culture, and economic development. Committees would operate by providing a venue for members to submit issues within the subject area that they wish to discuss in detail and introduce to the full assembly for initial debate. Once debated by the assembly for the first time, the motion would come back to the committee to consider amendments before being returned to the assembly for final debate (third reading) and vote.

Then comes the crucial referral stage. What happens to a motion passed by the Assembly of the Federation? This is where the institution would need to have some teeth. If passed by a majority in the assembly, a motion could be referred to provincial legislatures across the country to be either accepted or turned down by each provincial legislature. If a motion is accepted by a province, the premier and cabinet must strongly consider enacting legislation to address the motion. Alternatively, a motion passed by the assembly may be referred directly to the House of

Commons. These instances would likely be for issues of shared jurisdiction or broader issues spanning multiple provincial jurisdictions. This is where the assembly can make a significant contribution to the nation by drafting motions on national standards—for example, a motion to set national standards in health care, perhaps even national wait times.

Each week when the House of Commons is in session, a full day of debate is sometimes devoted to what is called Business of Supply, a technical term for what we normally call the "opposition day motion." On these days, one of the opposition parties will table a motion that either challenges government policy or brings forth an alternative opposition policy to be debated and voted upon. The result is not binding on the government but can elevate issues in the public eye and even pressure the prime minister to compromise on certain things. One of those days designated as Business of Supply could also entertain successful motions referred by the Assembly of the Federation. It is safe to say that an issue already supported by provincial representatives from across the country warrants serious consideration for debate and legislation in Ottawa as well as in our provincial capitals.

Conclusion

You may recall my opening description of the enthusiastic Standing Committee on Canadian Heritage debate about a bold, new, comprehensive program to teach our kids Canadian history. Our discussion came to a swift conclusion when we were reminded of provincial jurisdiction—such a lost opportunity. If only I could have intervened at that point and beaten back the tired, old jurisdictional refrain by pointing out that the Assembly of the Federation had passed a motion calling for a national history program for classrooms, and it was our responsibility as a federal government to make that happen. So much in our country is lost in the great divide between federal and provincial governments. Sharing of best practices, too, often goes unrealized because we never get to have an honest debate between provincial legislatures and Ottawa parliamentarians. When an issue arises among the provinces, our federal government mostly neglects and ignores them because doing otherwise would be too cumbersome or too contentious.

Our premiers are always quick to cry foul, saying that Ottawa must not dare interfere with provincial jurisdiction. But wouldn't it be a help to them to receive collective direction and advice from backbench politicians across the country? Perhaps they could feel free to harness brave, new ideas with the backing of their own members and not just their cabinets. Canada punches far above its weight on the international stage, but sometimes we must stop and reflect to gain a better understanding of ourselves. Our provincial MLAS, MPPS, MNAS and MHAS hold an incredible amount of knowledge at the very grassroots of our communities. It is time for us to include them in a national forum that improves our nation. We truly need—and can have—a house of sober *first* thought.

Conclusion

Michael Chong, Scott Simms and Kennedy Stewart

All of the contributors to this book are passionate about both the idea of democracy and its details, and have here attempted to convey the urgent need to reform or at least fine-tune Canada's democratic machinery. We are all concerned about over-centralization within our political parties, how some types of citizens are under-represented in the House of Commons, and how the place where it would seem to be most important to have space for discourse has become a badly scripted play that no one seems to want to watch or participate in.

Opportunities for change sometimes look bleak. For example, over the course of writing this book we went from having Prime Minister Justin Trudeau state, "The 2015 election will be the last federal election using first-past-the-post" to his abandoning this promise and instead "moving forward in a way that will focus on the things that matter to Canadians." In addition, Ed Broadbent observes that Donald Trump's rise to power has many wringing their hands about the current and future state of what some call the world's oldest democracy.

But there are also glimmers of hope. For example, when Trudeau was still committed to electoral reform in 2015, he struck the House of Commons Special Committee on Electoral Reform (ERRE). Rather than following traditional procedures and giving his majority government the majority of votes on ERRE (six Liberal, three Conservative and one NDP member), Trudeau opted to adopt NDP committee member Nathan Cullen's motion to decentralize control of this special committee composed of twelve members: five Liberals, three Conservatives, two New Democrats, one Bloc Québécois, and one Green. This meant that any recommendations would have to be made through compromise.

Between its creation in December 2015 and dissolution in December 2016, ERRE heard from thousands of Canadians and scores of experts about all aspects of Canada's democracy. Of the thirteen recommendations included in its final report, ten were dead on arrival. Four recommendations concerning a referendum on proportional representation have been rejected outright by the Liberal government. Four recommendations were merely symbolic, including vague commitments to make the voting process more accessible, improving voter turnout and engaging in future study of Canada's governance system. And two concerned rejecting mandatory election participation and online voting opportunities.

However there is a possibility that the three remaining recommendations could be acted upon by the Trudeau Liberals.

First, ERRE recommended the Canada Elections Act be amended to create a financial incentive (for example, through reimbursement of electoral campaign expenses) for political parties to run more women candidates and move toward parity in their nominations. This would go some ways to addressing concerns raised in this book by Anita Vandenbeld and move toward ensuring women hold more than their current 26 percent of the seats in the House of Commons.

Second, the committee recommended exploring ways in which youth under eighteen years old could be registered in the National Register of Electors up to two years in advance of reaching voting age. Allowing partial participation in elections at a younger age would increase citizen knowledge and could improve the very low youth-voter turnout rates.

Finally, the twelve members of ERRE agreed that Elections Canada should be empowered to encourage greater voter participation through initiatives such as mock student votes and advertising. These measures are again targeted at disengaged youth and those who normally do not vote in elections. These latter two measures could go some ways to addressing issues raised by Niki Ashton concerning how to politically empower young Canadians.

The glass-half-empty view would see ERRE as a failure in that it failed to convince the government to hold a referendum on bringing some form of proportional representation to Canada. The half-full view would point out that this extraordinary effort produced at least three actionable efforts that would address concerns raised in this book. Perhaps action can be taken on these measures after the smoke has cleared from the electoral-system reform debate.

The debate around electoral reform also produced other hopeful results. For example, an e-petition calling on the government to "immediately, declare its on-going commitment to ensuring the 2015 election be the last Federal Canadian election under the First Past the Post system" received over 130,000 signatures—the most of any e-petition in the just over fourteen months Canadians have been able to post and sign official petitions online. Regardless of what response the government emails back, that an e-petition has crossed the 100,000 threshold suggests the program is starting to become ingrained as a legitimate part of our democratic process. An earlier e-petition condemning all forms of Islamophobia was signed by almost 70,000 Canadians, reinforcing this idea.

E-petitioning started slowly in the United Kingdom but began to pick up steam as people saw the value in forcing the government to provide written responses to their demands. In fact, e-petitioning became so popular in the UK that the government changed the rules so the most popular e-petitions are now debated in the UK House of Commons. That e-petitions reaching a certain signature threshold would trigger a parliamentary debate was part of the original proposal for Canada's system suggests this reform might eventually be enacted here as well. We'll soon find out, as the Standing Committee on Procedure and House Affairs is required to undertake a review of the e-petitioning system in spring 2018.

At this stage readers might be thinking that improving e-petitioning, allowing young people to register to vote when they are sixteen, expanding Elections Canada advertising and incentivizing political parties to field more women candidates will do little to address the major problems with our democracy discussed in this book. They would be right.

Canadian politicians need to do more to tackle twenty-first century challenges such as a declining mainstream media, growing distrust of formal politics, declining voter turnout and the rise of far-right, anti-democratic sentiment and parties around the world. We need to do more to address the ever-increasing centralization of power within political parties, so gloomily portrayed in Robert Michels's "iron law of oligarchy." We need to do more to ensure our democratic institutions better reflect the characteristics of our larger population. And, as Bob Rae suggests, we have to act to change the way we speak to one another. Otherwise we will continue with what we have—a group of mainly old, straight white males shouting scripted questions and answers across the House of Commons in order to retain their parliamentary seats and work their way up the party hierarchy.

So where to begin? If this Parliament has proven anything, it is that change will not come from party leadership teams—especially not the Prime Minister's Office. Those who are able to secure power tend to favour institutions and rules that brought them that power. This includes MPs on both sides of the House.

Instead we'll likely need to follow the lead of the British Parliament and hope that backbench MPs will begin to act more in the interests of their constituents than the interests of their parties. This will not only come in the form of government backbenchers voting against bills and motions voting against their Prime Minister, but also opposition backbenchers defying the stranglehold of their leadership teams and sometimes voting with the government when interests align.

This new defiance will result in MPs being disciplined. Rebels will lose ministries or opposition critic portfolios, committee appointments and party positions as well as the accompanying salary boost. They will not be allocated questions in the House or receive media support from leadership teams. In extreme cases MPs will either step away from their caucuses, be kicked out to sit as independents or be taken out during local nomination contests. Forcing change will bring pain for many MPs.

This new defiance will require MPs not on leadership teams to stop thinking of themselves as career politicians, but rather as temporary political leaders. Get elected, serve your constituents, focus on making Canada and Canadian parties less centralized and suffer the conse-quences. To do so, MPs will need to have another career to fall back on when their advancement within their party is curtailed or they get kicked out and lose an election. Currently some MPs have other career options, but many do not. Those with fewer career choices become dependent on, and accustomed to, the high salary, public accolades and media attention. In other words, they are rendered ineffective by the trappings of riches, fame and power. These trappings and fears of losing their political careers are real. Many former MPs are unemployed or under-employed either due to a lack of marketable skills or because employers are reluctant to hire people with overtly partisan affiliations.

MPs will become empowered once they begin to think of their role in the machinery of national governance as a temporary position. They can then use their time in office to improve our democratic institutions for future generations. They can propose and vote for private member's bills and motions that empower regular MPs. They can fight within their own caucuses for leadership teams to decentralize power and lessen the power of the whip. As tough as this will be, it does appear that it is the only way reform happens—apart from rare and massive public protests.

Who knows? Maybe the most defiant MPs will defy the odds and be re-elected as independents because of these activities, or they may be picked up by rival parties wishing to project a more democratic image.

This book contains suggestions as to what these private member's bills might look like. For example, we could follow Elizabeth May's idea that some votes should only pass if they secure support from a super-majority of MPs. This would curtail a majority government's ability to ram its preferred bills and motions through the House and would instead require compromise to secure support from MPs in other parties. In addition, motions could be drafted to change the standing orders as they pertain to Michael Cooper's suggestions regarding Question Period, Michael Chong's committee representation reforms and my ideas to improve electronic petitioning and the amount of time dedicated to private members' business. Likewise, a special committee could be struck to examine Scott Simms's novel proposal for an Assembly of the Federation.

It is best to conclude by recalling Preston Manning's preferential "sign to Sawridge" metaphor. Perhaps Manning is correct and our governmental institutions used to point the way to democratic nirvana, but they need realignment to reflect massive and rapid technological and social changes that have occurred since Confederation. Or perhaps the old sign is more accurate than we think, but we have just failed to follow it. After all, MPs in 1867 were much more independent, leaders much less powerful and parties less controlling.

One thing that is certain is that we need space to debate these questions, and that space has been largely absent in Canada. While parties worry about their own internal operations and survival, there has really been no organization dedicated to impartially evaluating our democracy. This task has been largely taken up by the Hansard Society in the UK. Founded in 1944, the Hansard Society is an independent, non-partisan political research and education charity devoted to offering evidence-based ideas for reform of political and parliamentary institutions, processes and culture largely funded by Parliament and donations. We hope that Samara Canada, founded in 2009, can move to fulfill this role even more than it does now, but we realize it needs more support. Thus, all proceeds from this book will go to Samara, so that it can continue to create the space we need for these types of discussions.

Contributors

Niki Ashton is the member of Parliament for the riding of Churchill–Keewatinook Aski. First elected in 2008, she is a member of the NDP, the party's Critic for Jobs, Employment and Workforce Development and was a candidate in the 2012 leadership race.

Michael Chong has represented the riding of Wellington–Halton Hills since 2004. He served in the cabinet of Prime Minister Stephen Harper as Minister of Intergovernmental Affairs and Minister of Sport and was a contestant in the 2017 Conservative leadership race.

Michael Cooper, Conservative Party, was elected to represent the riding of St. Albert–Edmonton in 2015. He is the Official Opposition Deputy Critic for Justice.

NDP MP **Nathan Cullen** has represented Skeena–Bulkley Valley since 2004. He has held various senior portfolios for the NDP including House Leader and Finance Critic and stood as a candidate in the 2012 NDP leadership race.

Elizabeth May is the leader of the Green Party of Canada. She became the first Green Party candidate to be elected to the House of Commons in 2011 and represents the riding of Saanich–Gulf Islands.

Scott Simms is the member of Parliament for the Newfoundland and Labrador riding of Coast of Bays–Central–Notre Dame. First elected in 2004, he is a member of the Liberal Party and the current chair of the Standing Committee of Fisheries and Oceans.

Kennedy Stewart was elected in 2011 and is the NDP MP for Burnaby South. He is currently the NDP Critic for Science and chair of the NDP's British Columbia caucus.

Anita Vandenbeld is a member of the Liberal Party and was elected to represent the riding of Ottawa West–Nepean in 2015. She is a member of the Standing Committee of the Status of Women and chaired the Special Committee on Pay Equity in 2016.

Index